THE FINAL
FREEDOM

DOUGLAS WEISS, PH.D.

Requests for information should be addressed to:

Discovery Press
P.O. Box 51055, Colorado Springs, CO 80949
719-278-3708

Library of Congress Cataloging-in-Publication Data

Weiss, Douglas.
The Final Freedom: Pioneering Sexual Addiction Recovery /
Douglas W.Weiss
p. cm.
Discovery Press, 1998
ISBN 1-881292-37-1
1. Sex Addiction--Treatment. I.Title
97-91762
CIP

Edited by Elizabeth Prestwood
Interior designed by Jamie Dodd
Cover designed by Janelle Evangelides
Printed in the United States of America

DEDICATION

This book is dedicated to my lovely wife, Lisa, who has accompanied me on my journey to the final freedom, and to all those who take this brave journey for themselves.

CONTENTS

INTRODUCTION

The final freedom is a place beyond the guilt and shame of the history of sexual addiction. It is a place we reach after hard work and humility, where we begin to see the light of becoming human. The feeling of becoming human is what we experience after we are aware of our sexual addiction--and it is quite a miracle to behold.

I have participated in this great journey to the final freedom personally, and I admire and applaud countless others who are on their own journey. For me, the journey was difficult. It was full of many days of hard work and fear of the addiction itself. But the process of admitting I was sexually addicted was the first step of hope on a long road to a place of living free.

Traveling this journey required being humble and honest. I needed to "thaw out" my feelings and allow others through what I call "the glass wall" that protected me. The journey required telling all, so that I could be freed from the lie, "If you really knew me, you wouldn't love me." I had to be honest about the abuses, neglects and abandonments in my past. I bravely searched into my family tree and found others who were afflicted with this same addiction--only during their generation it was yet to be labeled or identified as treatable.

All of this had to be accomplished so I could now experience friendship, serenity, intimacy--and the psychological and spiritual stability--that are part of the wonderful journey toward the final freedom.

Your journey will uniquely be yours alone. It may prove to be just as intense, and just as rewarding. But it will be worth every step.

Though this journey is the most difficult in the beginning as you arrest your thoughts and behaviors and begin to live life honestly, it will become easier as you share the load with others who care enough to embark on such a brave trip with you.

This book is written to help the brave-hearted person who dares to take the journey to understand the addiction they have, for whatever reason they have it. It is my intent that this book serve as only one tool in a process, which may require many, for you to reach your final destination. I hope the following pages make your recovery easier, and help you reach the final freedom.

Douglas Weiss, Ph.D.

PART ONE
ASPECTS OF SEXUAL ADDICTION

IT'S TIME TO HEAL

1

In the 1930s, the American culture began to deal with alcohol as an addiction. Alcoholics Anonymous was formed and The Twelve Step Program was created. In the 1970s we began to address drug addiction in relation to this. In the 80s, the medical profession studied addictions to food and gambling. Today we appear to be at the start of a serious movement looking into sexual addiction and its recovery. There is an openness to address it that we haven't experienced before--and yet there are still misconceptions. For example, it is interesting to me that a culture such as ours will put almost any type of sexual behavior on television, but will add a disclaimer warning "not for young audiences" on a show that talks straight about sexual addiction. What a contradiction! (I actually experienced this as a guest on talk shows dealing with sexual addiction).

Looking beyond this contradiction, the medical and psychological communities are finally opening up to the reality of sexual addiction. Sexual addiction and other addictive behaviors have been observed for as long as recorded history. It took quite a while for people to progress from seeing alcoholics as drunks who can't hold their liquor, to persons who have a disease that is now treatable. Currently, it is almost vogue to be recovering from "something," whether it be alcohol, drugs or shopping!

I believe we are in the early stages of understanding sex addiction in our culture. In one television studio audience where I was a guest, when asked if they had heard of sex addiction, 25 percent of the people raised their hands. At a speaking engagement in a major university, I asked how many had heard of sex addiction. Again, I received a 25 percent show of hands. So I believe we are making a lot of progress in sex addiction awareness.

Because I believe sex addiction transcends cultures, I want to broaden the concept of sex addiction as being merely an American phenomenon to being known as a worldwide reality. Years ago, I placed a home page on the Internet. I offered information about sex addiction and ways to obtain books and additional material. The response was incredible! And still is. I receive tens of thousands of visitors every month from almost every nation in the world.

There are sex addicts in almost every country. This is not an American problem but a worldwide problem. Fortunately, just like alcoholism, it can be treated, and people can be restored to sanity no matter what language they speak or in what culture they live. We live in an exciting time when people are seeking help for their addiction--and for the first time, help is available.

What this may mean to you as you read this book is simple. When you go to a Twelve Step Meeting for sexual addiction in a large town and see only six people there, you don't have to be concerned. In the 1930s Alcoholics Anonymous began exactly the same way. Things changed then, and they are changing now. The groups may be small now, but they won't stay that way.

Many who start this journey toward sex addiction recovery are pioneers. As pioneers, we are the first to taste the fruit of recovery from sex addiction, before the rest of the culture does. And we get to pave the way for others in how to deal with those who don't understand. Because as a pioneer, you may often be misunderstood by others who have not yet come to understand the plight and the prevalence of sex addiction, and the devastation it can cause.

As I see it, you are starting to move toward--a pioneer along on your journey toward freedom from sexual addiction. Few have gone before you, but many will come after you. As a pioneer, you are the future leader of this movement. As you get thirty or ninety days of recovery behind you, and then eventually years of recovery, you will have gained experience and understanding of a disease that very few understand including those in the professional field. Many, I believe, who are starting their recovery from sex addiction today will be tomorrow's future experiential experts in this freedom movement. The current possible misunderstandings of what you are doing today will make sense to others years from now--and the journey will have been worth it for your sake and countless others.

I personally started my journey twenty-one years ago, and I am thankful that I did. I not only have been given the gift of many years of sobriety without relapse, but I, by grace, have been able to expose the topic of sex addiction and freedom from it to millions of people. I didn't know this was my future when I was working on my early recovery and healing from past sexual abuse, neglect and abandonment issues.

Was being misunderstood and having to feel the pain worth it? YES! Today I have the opportunity to see others reach final freedom as they hear this message and respond to the healing process from sex addiction. Their choice to go the journey makes my recovery and the boundaries I must keep to maintain my sobriety very worthwhile. One life like yours or mine can help many people begin and maintain recovery from sex addiction.

Guilt and shame are common feelings in early recovery, but as you move forward and begin to get first thirty and then ninety days of sobriety behind you, and actively pursue the steps, I find that most people begin to see and feel the guilt and shame break away. This is especially true after completing Step Five.

There is no shame in being a recovering sex addict just like there is no shame being a recovering "anything." Of all the people who could have taken responsibility for their lives and behaviors, you have. I used to ask God, "Why me? Why am I an addict?" Now I ask Him, "Why did You choose me, out of the millions who suffer and die from this disease, to get freedom?"

I have no shame about being a recovering sex addict. My father didn't know he had this disease and neither did anyone else in my family. I am the first one who had a chance at recovering and helping stop this disease from moving down my family tree any further. You may be the first in your entire lineage to acknowledge this disease. Recovering from sex addiction may be one of the largest contributions you will leave your future generations. I am proud of your efforts in considering this journey. There is more and more hope for you in each step that you take.

Realizing you are a sex addict is only the beginning of the long journey. This journey will definitely be adventurous as you discover how to live a life of sobriety with intimacy, trust, fun and healthy relationships. This is just the beginning--and as you see others take the same journey toward wholeness, you also will be changed for a lifetime. The world needs brave pioneers in sexual addiction recovery to go through to the final freedom. Welcome to the journey.

BIOLOGICAL ASPECTS

2

Just like other addictions, sexual addiction is multifaceted. It isn't caused by any singular reason. Its roots can be found in many possible areas.

Much like alcoholism was in its earlier days; sexual addiction has been viewed as a moral problem. The thought has been, "If the addict would just control himself, he wouldn't act this way." Too often sexual addiction has been cast as a character or spiritual problem. Many people have labeled it a psychological problem. The real root of sexual addiction isn't any one factor. And discovering the root to your personal addiction requires a study of the possible causes. To begin our study, let's examine what I call the missing link--the biological aspect.

The biological aspect is often the missing piece for sex addicts who are in the early stages of recovery. It offers hope and explanations to those who have searched elsewhere for answers. For example, many sex addicts have tried spiritual solutions, such as praying, without experiencing any improvement in their sexual behavior. Others who have grown up in fairly healthy homes having had no psychological trauma or abuse are confused as to why they are sexually addicted. Sex addicts who have explored these areas with no results find the biological component is often the missing link they have been searching for.

There are several biological aspects of sex addiction. But before we can begin to grapple with the biological and neurological aspects of sex addiction, we first must have a brief discussion about the brain.

The brain is an organ just like the lungs and heart. Organs have needs, including chemical needs that must be met. Endorphins and enkephalins are two of the chemicals that the brain needs. Everyone has the need for these chemicals. As a part of its developmental tasks, the brain is driven to get this need met. The brain can get these endorphins and enkephalins in several different ways. Running or high aerobic activity can be one of the ways which the brain receives these two chemicals, resulting in what is known as the "runner's high." A lot of research has been done on the runner's high. This "high" feeling is a neurological buzz or a flood of endorphins and enkephalins which I term "brain cookies." The runner gets to a place during his run in which his body is in enough pain that his brain gets flooded with endorphins and enkephalins--which together create an opiate-type substance that creates a buzz. Consequently, it is something the brain will begin to want again and again.

The brain can also get these chemical needs met through creativity, expression, intimacy or connecting with another person. The brain doesn't necessarily distinguish between right and wrong. It is only focused on getting its neurological needs met.

Let's look at these in a paradigm. Picture the brain as having six or seven small pipes through which the endorphin and enkephalin chemicals enter. The diameter of each pipe determines the quantity of chemicals that flow through it. A pipe with a wide diameter allows more through than a narrow one. Consequently, if we were athletic in our past, that small pipe may be a little wider than others. If we were not very artistic, that pipe would stay small. If we had never had intimacy in our past or present, that pipe would stay very small. Then when we do become sexual, we send a lot of endorphins and enkephalins to the brain. These chemicals are powerful substances that flood the brain.

Sex addicts consistently report that over time, they are sexual many more times than they are artistic, intimate or athletic. And as they grow older, the sexual acting out becomes more and more regular whether it is with themselves, others or both. From regularly acting out sexually, that particular pipe can become the greatest way the brain gets its neurological needs met. Now the brain isn't discerning as to whether this pathway is moral or immoral. It is simply an organ that wants its "brain cookies." If acting out sexually is the primary way to get these "cookies," this may be the very reason why so many addicts have been unsuccessful in their treatment. Their problem really isn't all related to abuse, trauma or spirituality. It's biological. Most likely the sex addict hasn't looked at the neurological aspects that may need reconditioning.

Let's consider another paradigm. Let's now say the brain has a new pathway similar to a freshly cut out dirt road. That dirt road, after being traveled on many times becomes a highway. By the time the sex addict comes for counseling, that sexual behavior pathway is much like the autobahn in order for his brain to receive its brain cookies. Acting out sexually has become the primary way this person has conditioned his brain to get its chemical needs met. Many sex addicts understand this reality and the repetition of it. Part of their recovery is learning to balance these neurological pathways or dirt roads. This will be an important part of the final freedom recovery puzzle as we talk about retraining the brain in a later chapter in this book.

Neurological Conditioning

Most of us are familiar with the story of Pavlov's dog. You may have learned about classic conditioning in Psych 101. You may remember that Pavlov's dog was given food after a bell was rung. Over a period of time, the dog connected the bell with the food so much, that when the bell would ring, he would begin to salivate--thus, a biological response. This can also happen with humans. For example, all of us have run out of school when the bell was rung for recess. I can remember sitting in class at school just waiting for that bell to ring. I had a conditioned response to that bell. I knew when the bell rang, I got to get up and go play.

A sex addict's conditioned response works the same way. The neurological conditioning is incredible. Most sex addicts who have sexual behaviors with others also have some kind of thought patterns to go along with them. I call this an altered state. Conditioning is usually connected to an altered state. An altered state, otherwise known as fantasy, is a place sex addicts go mentally to escape reality. In this place, a sex addict feels loved, important, and significant. Of course everyone in this fantasy world are objects who do everything the addict wants them to do. The neurological conditioning occurring is actually a sexual conditioning because sexual needs are getting met, but only because they are connecting to something else. What the sexual conditioning is connecting to is the altered state experience.

When the addict goes into the altered state experience, the brain expects and demands an ejaculation. This fantasy world begins with many addicts at a young age of 13 or 14 years old. Your body will have physiological responses to whatever sexual thoughts you put in your altered state. Many addicts have connected their neurological and biological conditioning to objects that look a certain way in their fantasy world. Some have specific preferences such as body proportions or a particular hair and eye color combination. Whatever fantasies have been put into the altered state, the addict will pursue. This is a classic conditioning process. Many wives can sense when their husbands go into this altered state and consequently they often feel they are alone during sex. This is because the addict has emotionally checked out on them.

Before recovery, the sex addict goes into this altered state thousands and thousands of times during intercourse or while being sexual with himself because he has conditioned himself to altered state sex. This is quite different from relational sex. Many addicts have reported to me that they have had sexual experiences in the altered state hundreds or thousands of times before they even had their first sexual experience with another person. This is why sex addicts get quite irritated at their partner when they experience resistance of any type from their partner sexually. Their past sexual conditioning has been in their altered state, "Whatever I want, I get it whenever I want it." You can see how the neurological conditioning process is a very important part of sexual addiction and will also be important in the recovery as well.

When the sex addict is triggered by a fantasy he has put into his altered state, he begins to sexually salivate, sort of like Pavlov's dog. If redheaded females are in the sex addict's fantasy world, and he sees a redheaded female in reality, he will feel pulled in that direction. This is because of the neurological, biological, and sexual conditioning of the sex addict. It is for this reason that early in recovery, the sex addict must identify his "trigger group" because this specific group of people will solicit a neurological, biological and sexual response when the addict is confronted by it. It is not a cognitive response when the addict spots his trigger group. It often happens in a microsecond and he finds himself in a dilemma. This dilemma has nothing to do with the sex addict's partners. It has to do with the conditioning the addict has done to himself.

Neurological conditioning, if not addressed in treatment, can be the fall of many sex addicts. We will talk later about the spiritual and psychological aspects which can set up a reason for the behavior. For example, there may not have been intimacy in your family and you were emotionally deprived while growing up. You may have found that acting out sexually was a way of meeting your needs emotionally. While you were acting out sexually, you were beginning to condition yourself neurologically. So even if you address some of the other issues you have had, you still have a neurological conditioning aspect that you will need to address to achieve sobriety in your recovery.

I have heard that the brain is the largest sexual organ we have. I have come to the conclusion from the thousands of sex addicts I have counseled with, this is true. What the addict has done with his brain has caused a neurological reality. This reality cannot be ignored and must be evaluated and treated for what it is. We have heard the saying "once an alcoholic, always an alcoholic." This may be more neurological than anything else. The same is true for sexual addiction--the pathway may grow smaller again over a period of time. While we don't have enough information to make this conclusion, we do see people who have longer periods of sobriety, who struggle a lot less. The addict may need to create new pathways, learn to have relational sex, and retrain his brain.

He needs to learn how to have his brain become a partner in his recovery, rather than an enemy. Alcoholics Anonymous has a saying called "Stinking Thinking." I interpret this during recovery as the neurological needs of the brain saying, "What are you doing? We have done this behavior for 35 years. Why stop something that is working?" From a neurological perspective, your brain has developed this particular method to get its needs met. The sex addict has reinforced this method by acting out sexually. The brain cannot distinguish whether this is an appropriate or inappropriate method. But the sex addict knows that the medicine eventually can become the problem and that he needs to recover from neurological, biological and sexual conditioning that his past has reinforced.

What we have learned about sex addiction over the last decade is that these brain chemicals hit the excitement centers in the prefrontal cortex. The prefrontal cortex is a part of the brain that develops into the mid to late twenties. This neuro-conditioning is occurring in "wet cement" during our adolescence. Also, the adrenal gland releases a chemical called peptin sealing this image into our brain. This is why many sex addicts can remember pornography from twenty to fifty years ago.

Research on the brain and sex is still continuing. If this subject interests you, it is covered in great detail in the AASAT (American Association for Sex Addiction Therapy) class that you can take by going to www.aasat.org.

Needless to say, our brain is a significant piece in understanding sexual addiction. As you take the journey of the final freedom even your brain gets better, at least that's my experience observing sex addicts heal from their sexual addiction.

PSYCHOLOGICAL ASPECTS AND THE 6 TYPES

For some addicts, the psychological aspects have a great bearing on their sexual addiction. For other addicts these may be the second or third aspect of their sexual addiction. Many sex addicts who have sought treatment at inpatient facilities report that they have come from abusive backgrounds including physical, sexual and spiritual abuse and neglect. In this chapter we will focus on these abuses and neglects.

Abandonment

Abandonment is experienced not exclusively but primarily in the family of origin. I believe it was the Creator's purpose that a child be cared for and nurtured in the family unit. Yet in our culture, abandonment issues are greater than they have ever been. This is especially evident in the 20th Century because of increasingly high divorce rates.

Personally I have never met my biological father. My legal father and mother divorced when I was young and I grew up in many foster homes. Losing a primary figure in life due to death or divorce can be unimaginably painful and confusing for a child. The need for both parents throughout the years of childhood is very strongly supported in research literature. When those needs for two parents go unmet, the consequences of emotional pain can set a person up for some form of compulsivity. Although this is not limited to sexual addiction, it is one of the first addictions an adolescent can experience before alcohol and drugs become available. It can often be the first medication for the pain of abandonment.

Abuse

Abuse is another aspect many sex addicts report as a root to their addiction. Let's discuss the various kinds of abuse that can occur in the development of a child.

Physical abuse - Being slapped in the face inappropriately or being hit excessively and/or inappropriately with or without explanation is a form of physical abuse. Some people have grown up where one parent had an addiction and when that parent was in the midst of their addiction, he or she abused them. Flashbacks of being hurt, abused and violated in a physical sense make a child question his safety. Children who have lived in these circumstances will also question their self worth, because the primary care giver violated and abused them, instead of providing a caring relationship.

Emotional abuse - Emotional abuse occurs by shaming and making children overly responsible for their behavior. Inappropriate age development tasks for children are emotional abuse. These behaviors cause pain for the developing child and his family system can predispose him or her to choosing a form of addiction to act out in order to medicate the pain.

Spiritual abuse - Spiritual abuse is when spirituality is used in this situation as a mood-altering state as opposed to a living relationship with God. There appears to be a great difference in people who approach God relationally compared with those who approach Him as an object. Some sex addicts have grown up in families in which they were forced into a belief system and shamed for questioning the system. They were unable to explore spirituality for themselves and consequently shamed with religious language for having any sexuality. We are all sexual beings by nature and yet in a religiously addictive system, you can be shamed, ostracized or humiliated for wanting sexual information.

Sexual Abuse - This is an abuse that can be overwhelming to the spirit, soul and body of a human being. It is an abuse that violates the inner core of who a person is. Research shows that sexual abuse can set you up for sexual preoccupation such as an early fantasy life, and acting out sexually, or completely shutting down sexually. The list can go on and on as to the effects of sexual abuse. Children have very few skills to be able to process or deal with sexual abuse. This abuse forces a child into an adult world that he or she is not ready for cognitively, in feelings or choices. When the reality of the abuse comes to light, it is very painful. Often sexual abuse occurrences may not be remembered by a victim until after they are further into their recovery and memories they have suppressed from early childhood suddenly begin to surface.

The sex addict's sexual abuse could have been perpetrated by either gender. There are cultural misconceptions that sex with an older female and a younger male (such as 12 year-old boy and a 16 year-old girl) is not sexual abuse, and that it should be a positive experience. This is simply not true. One sex addict who came to my office told me that when he was 13 years old, he went to his friend's house to play. His friend wasn't there but the boy's mother invited him in and engaged in sexual behavior with him. This behavior continued until the day before his wedding at age 30. He could not allow himself to believe that this experience with his friend's mother was sexual abuse. He was referred to me because he was suffering from major depression. When I counseled him, he was having seven affairs at one time and couldn't handle it. There was a direct link for him between his abuse and sexual addiction.

Sexual abuse pushes the victim into experiencing sex as a sexual object and to objectify sexuality. This experience creates a need to medicate to escape the pain. Sexual addiction can be one of those medications.

Unlike the situation where the man engaged in sexual behavior with his friend's mom, some people are sexually abused through a homosexual experience. The effects of this type of abuse can cause several different behaviors. Some people have had to wrestle with sexual identity questions. Others felt they had to prove to themselves that they were not homosexual, and thus they may have compulsively acted out sexually with females. Having a homosexual experience as a first experience can bring much confusion and cause an individual to act out either heterosexually to avoid grappling with the issue of being homosexual, or to act out homosexually to confirm that this indeed is the behavior of their choice since it is the only one they may have experienced.

Sexual abuse can affect the sex addict not only in choosing an addiction to medicate the pain, but also in choosing specific sexual behaviors due to the confusion the abuse caused.

Neglect

Our culture is finally recognizing neglect as equally damaging as the traumas and abandonments that we have already discussed. Neglect is defined as the parents' irresponsibility of the child's development in any area.

Spiritual Neglect - Spiritual neglect is an absence of spiritual information and development. A child who is spiritually neglected often is not encouraged to connect with the concept of God and discussion about God may be totally absent from the home. This can leave a child feeling incomplete. Spiritual neglect can cause a child to feel unaccountable to God or even to himself.

Physical Neglect - A child whose physical needs aren't met can set the child up for pain that eventually will need medication. Forms of physical neglect can include a child being humiliated by others because he or she does not have appropriate attire for school, not getting enough food to eat or not receiving adequate nutrition. It can be in the form of being physically abandoned by the parents for several days at a time. A physically neglected child can be deprived of necessary medical treatment. These physical neglects can be just as traumatizing as some of the physical abuses, and in some cases both neglects and abuses are occurring at the same time. The combination of neglect and abuse only compound the pain many sex addicts experienced growing up.

Emotional neglect - The following is a metaphor that is useful in understanding what emotional neglect can do, especially in one's early development.

I believe the human being has a sponge inside that needs water on a regular basis. This sponge is their individuality, personhood, and the way that they see themselves. The water the sponge needs is approval, praise, encouragement and affirmation. Many who have grown up in dysfunctional families can quickly conclude that their sponge was never watered. They have a sense of emotional deprivation. Their sponge just got drier and drier because they didn't know how to ask for their needs to be met. They were not the adult in the situation. Now, as an adult, there is an internal ache in their inner being, and it stems from the emotional neglect. One or both parents may have been distant or emotionally absent. Recovery can actually be the very first experience they have in receiving praise, affirmation from someone. Everyone needs to hear praise, affirmation and encouragement--and we don't need to be ashamed of this need.

If you were emotionally neglected, as you move along in your recovery, you will realize that you don't need to be ashamed that you need to receive emotional support and encouragement. The dryness inside that needs to be medicated in your addiction has been set up early in life. Addiction has provided a place for emotional nurturance through creating a world of fantasy--a world that is nurturing and encouraging. In some addicts' lives, these sexual fantasies were their first partner. This often was the safest place to go where they could escape the emotional absence in their home environment and gain some kind of emotional support, even though it was a false place. Giving up sex addiction is not only about giving up being sexual in inappropriate ways, but often it is giving up the first caring relationship that the sex addict may have experienced. This false relationship has been primary and is what has helped the addict get through life. In light of all this information, it is easy to see how addiction is definitely something that may have replaced the emotional neglect a person suffered.

Sexual Neglect - There is little that American literature has to say about sexual neglect, even though it is a very common phenomenon. Many of us have experienced growing up in a family where we received little or no sexual information from our parents. Research shows that most sexual information adults received when they were children came from peers who knew just as little about sex as they did.

Sexual neglect is the old rule where we don't talk about it even though most are experiencing it. Sexual neglect can breed confusion and unnatural inquiry while trying to identify and relate to an expression of our own sexuality.

One sex addict said that he grew up where sex was a dirty and bad thing, and you were to save it for the one you love. This is quite an ironic message: The person you love the most, you give the most disgusting gift to. This is a message that many of us received in our growing up years.

Others reported learning from other sources. Some have said they received pornography as their sexual education from one of their parents. The bottom line in these situations is, someone who is deprived of sexual information has only their own childlike investigative procedures to solve their internal development problems.

Sexual neglect can not only be found in sexual addicts' backgrounds, but also in co-addicts' backgrounds. It is very important in recovery to gain back appropriate sexual information a person has been deprived of earlier in life--even though many sex addicts may think they have a lot of sexual information. Most sex addicts lack basic understanding of sexual behavior and the way the sexual system works.

Sexual neglect can set the addict up to medicate the absence in their development. As we talk about these neglects and abuses, you will see that each one can set up a cavity in the soul of the addict that needs filling, explaining and interacting. If this pain goes untreated, over time it will become more intense and will drive the addict to find solace somewhere. Some find solace in alcohol, drugs or sex. These psychological issues can be the primary cause of sexual addiction for some, and for others it can be a secondary cause. As a holistic approach to sexual addiction, I believe that the psychological aspects of addiction are very important for each sex addict to consider and investigate during their recovery journey.

There are four other types of sex addicts in addition to the Biological addict and the Psychological addict that we have already highlighted. Here I'll address the 6 Types of Sex Addicts briefly including the ones that we already talked about so that you can have a cohesive list of all the types.

The 6 Types of Sex Addicts

It's been more than 20 years ago now since I have treated my first sex addicted client. In the early years many paradigms of understanding and treating sex addicts were the best guess at the time.

As a field we have grown considerably. As a clinician and now a psychologist, I have looked into the souls of many sex addicts and I have discovered not all sex addicts are alike. Intuitively when an addict attends a support group they also realize they are not alike as well.

Here, I want to share with you a paradigm that I, and my clients, have found very helpful. I will cover the six types of sex addicts briefly. I go into greater detail on the CD's The 6 Types of Sex Addicts and the follow up CD, Treatment for the 6 Types of Sex Addicts. This subject and application is also available on several hours of DVDs in the training offered by the AASAT (American Association for Sex Addiction Therapists).

1 THE BIOLOGICAL SEX ADDICT

In chapter two we discussed the biological components to sex addiction. This biological reinforcement creating neuropathways to pleasure glues the addict to object relationship sex (porn, fantasy, or disconnected sex with people).

Almost all sex addicts have a biological component. In my experience, less than 15 percent are only biological sex addicts. This would mean the other five types do not apply to them.

In a solely biological sex addict, he or she typically grew up in relatively healthy homes and had no sexual or other type of trauma. The addict simply created the neuroconditioning cycle in a steady manner leading them to sexual addiction.

2 THE PSYCHOLOGICAL SEX ADDICT

Generally in research related to sexual addiction the larger population of sex addicts have suffered some form of abuse or neglect. This person finds the combination of the messages in the fantasy world and the sexual chemical cock-tail to the brain to be a salve unto their hurting soul. Simply put, they medicate the past or the pain in their souls with acting out which is their form of medicine.

In my clinical experience, 80 percent or more have abandonment, abuse or neglect issues of some type in their past. These painful events will ultimately need to be addressed for the addict to fully heal.

3 THE SPIRITUAL BASED SEX ADDICT

This addict is looking for a spiritual connection in all the wrong places. In recovery we talk about our spiritual hole. This person puts sex in this hole and finds it doesn't scratch the itch over time.

He or she may have a spiritual awakening of some type and the sexual behaviors that were addictive cease. They filled their hole and now pursue sex in a healthy manner.

Every addict wishes this was their experience. I have worked with medicine men, new agers, Muslims, Hindus, Rabbis, Pastors and Priests, all who had a spiritual experience but still maintained their sexual addiction. I understand this personally and still had to do the healing work after my spiritual awakening to heal from my own sexual addiction.

4 THE TRAUMA BASED SEX ADDICT

The trauma based sex addict has experienced sexual trauma(s) as a child or adolescent. This trauma becomes the major repetitive behavior in his sexual addiction.

If the addict has experienced a particular trauma then this trauma behavior becomes the addict's predominant fantasy, porn selection and reenactment in his sex addiction. As in the case we discussed earlier, the 13 year-old boy who is sexually abused by a 30 year-old married woman which continues past high school repeats this behavior by having multiple affairs of a consistent theme. All of his affairs included women who were 15 years or more older than him.

For the trauma based sex addict the trauma determines the flavor of the sexual addiction. Here trauma work will need to be address for the addict to heal.

5 THE INTIMACY ANOREXIC SEX ADDICT

In earlier research we determined 29 percent of sex addicts fit into the category of intimacy anorexia. This subject is covered in great detail in the Intimacy Anorexia DVD as well as the DVD for the spouse of the sex addict called Married and Alone.

To be brief, I will list the characteristics of intimacy anorexia. Answer these the way your spouse or partner would answer them about you. If you believe that five or more criteria apply to you, then you are probably an intimacy anorexic.

1. Withhold love
2. Withhold praise or appreciation
3. Control by silence/anger
4. Criticism causing isolation
5. Withholding sex
6. Blaming partner for everything
7. Staying very busy to avoid partner time
8. Control/Shame with money issues
9. Unable to share feelings
10. Withholding spiritual connection

Many addicts who have been trying to get sober but keep having what I call "flat tire" recovery (relapsing regularly) often are un-identified as intimacy anorexics. If you have been sober from sex-ual addictive acting out behaviors for a year but your wife wants to leave you now because "nothing's changed" you might also be a sexual/emotional anorexic.

THE SEX ADDICT WITH MOOD DISORDERS

Some sex addicts in adolescence or young adulthood have chemi-cal imbalances. This young person finds the sexual release as a way to medicate or alter their chemical imbalance. He then uses this sexual response quite regularly and over time creates a sexual addiction. In a journal article I wrote called The Prevalence of Depression in Male Sex Addicts Residing in the United States I discovered that 28% of male sex addicts suffered from depression.

A second common chemical imbalance that I see in my practice with sex addicts is Cyclothymic Disorder. This is a slight up and down in mood usually experienced by the clients as a funky day on a weekly or so basis. This type of sex addict will need to do all of the recovery work discussed here and in the 101 Practical Exercises in addition to seeing a psychiatrist for possible medica-tion for the mood disorder.

Can I be More Than One Type?

Absolutely! Most sex addicts come in groupings of several types. Once you know the type of sex addict you are then following a treatment plan for your type will be very beneficial for you.

Heart to Heart Counseling Center offers counseling. If you would like an assessment and treatment plan specific to your type(s) of sex addiction, call 719-278-3708. So many addicts are surprised at what they can learn about themselves in simply one hour. You can also download more information on the six types from our website www.sexaddict.com.

You really need to be fully informed when you start your recovery. Also your recovery affects so many people in your life. So continue to read the solution aspects of this book. I have been sober for more than 21 years without a relapse. You deserve the final freedom for your life as well!

THE "NEW" ADDICTION CYCLE

A New Perspective

During the past 20 years treating sexual addiction I noticed specific patterns appearing among the addicts in my practice. In the field of sexual addiction there have been several clinicians trying to define this trip the addict takes when moving from normal life toward the zone of the addiction.

How can a perfectly sane person repetitively choose sex addition behaviors against their better judgment? I know personally and professionally that there is a quantum leap between reality and addiction. Within the next few pages I will discuss a path many of us have traveled from sanity to insanity. I call this map to insanity the New Addiction Cycle.

We will first discuss the four broad aspects of pain agents: emotional discomfort, unresolved conflict, stress, and a need to connect. You can discover which of the four main pain agents relate to you, and then continue to determine what other of the many possible pain agents may apply to you in your life. These pain agents and others move the addict toward the next level of the addiction cycle.

THE "NEW" ADDICTION CYCLE

I. Pain Agents

   A. Emotional Discomfort
   B. Unresolved Conflict
   C. Stress
   D. A Need To Connect

II. Disassociation

III. The Altered State

IV. Pursuing Behavior

V. Behavior

VI. Time

I. Pain Agents

Most addicts, as we have discussed in previous chapters, have experienced biological, psychological and/or spiritual reasons for their sexual addiction. What I have experienced in working with sexual addicts is that there is a need to escape and not feel the pain they have experienced in the past. Many sex addicts have developed a coping mechanism to escape from the pain of a childhood and/or adolescent trauma. This coping mechanism for escape has carried the addict through most of his adult life. When things get difficult for the sex addict, he will do something to medicate the pain by taking an emotional aspirin (act out) to avoid dealing with the trauma from the past.

There are many pain agents, four of which we will discuss here, that move the addict into the beginning of the sexual addiction cycle. The beginning of this cycle often starts with a shameful experience. In recovery, when the addict begins to understand this cycle, he will be able to short circuit the necessity to act out.

A. Emotional Discomfort

Emotional discomfort is one of the primary pain agents that will move the addict to the first level of the addiction cycle and cause them to disconnect from their feelings. Emotional discomfort is basically a family of origin issue. The sex addict never learned how to identify feelings while growing up in his or her family. Consequently, many sex addicts have very primitive emotional skills. Therefore, when they have a painful feeling, they act out sexually to feel better. I remember knowing that when I felt any kind of emotional discomfort as an addict, whether it was hopelessness, anger or confusion, I couldn't quite put my finger on it to identify it. Whatever uncomfortable emotional feelings I had, I knew that if I just acted out in some way, it would go away temporarily. The interesting thing about this is, it worked! My addiction did medicate the emotional discomfort I was feeling temporarily. Emotional discomfort for many sex addicts is the pain agent that moves them forward into the next steps of the cycle of addiction.

B. Unresolved Conflict

Some sex addicts have been victims of physical, emotional or sexual abuse and have unresolved issues about the abuse(s). Some have unresolved conflicts about their sexual identity or goals in life. Any kind of unresolved external or internal conflict can agitate the addict. It is this agitation that becomes part of this particular pain agent's unresolved conflict. The sense that "I don't have that skill mastered yet," or "I don't feel good about myself because of that" can trigger the addict into the addiction cycle. These unresolved conflicts agitate the addict which is the beginning process for the cycle of addiction. An example of a trigger point for this unresolved conflict might be growing up in a physically abusive home and having unresolved issues around the abuse. When the addict has unresolved conflict, they act out as a way to avoid, minimize or medicate this conflict. This can show up in their personal or professional life. For example, the addict may have an argument or misunderstanding with someone at the office and act out as a way to make themselves feel better due to their unresolved conflict.

C. Stress

Something we cannot avoid is stress. All of us have stress at some point in our lives. The way a sex addict medicates or avoids stress, is by acting out. After acting out, the stress seems to dissipate. However, the fact that the sex addict acted out creates more stress that makes a cycle for them to keep adding stress to the pain agent and repeat the cycle. Many sex addicts set up these dynamics in which they repeat this behavior by creating stress so that they can alleviate the stress again by acting out.

Stress can be located in several areas in the addict's life. It can come from the realm of his vocation. It can be from the pressure of finances as many sex addicts have difficulty budgeting money. Stressors can be tied to close relationships, family of origin or children. It can be about spiritual issues. Just the everyday grind of driving through traffic can be stressful for some. Stress--pressure from outside--can move the addict into a pain agent and back into the cycle of addiction.

D. A Need to Connect

Every human being has a need to connect. I believe that everyone is born with a need to touch and be touched. Many sexual addicts act out sexually as a primary way of being satiated inside. It is through this altered state and false nurturing that the addict feels like he or she is connected. This can be very confusing for the sex addict in recovery since experiences of acting out in the past have all been a way to connect through his sexual addiction. This need to connect can move the addict into the addiction cycle if he doesn't find other ways to enjoy the true way of meeting the need to connect. I have found that when sexual addicts feel this need to connect, they also feel pain because they don't know how to get this relationship need met. The addict is faced with the pressure to act out in order to make the pain go away.

II. Disassociation

A common clinical term used in the treatment of addictions and traumas is disassociation. Disassociation simply means that the addict disconnects from himself. Many addicts disconnect while driving. They may find that they have drifted off into all kinds of thoughts and pictures, and sometimes it may be difficult to concentrate. Often the sexual addict works at jobs much lower than his skill level because he disassociates so frequently. Disconnecting is a way that many sexual abuse victims survive from the pain of their past. These victims most likely disconnected during their trauma as well. Disconnecting while growing up in a dysfunctional home may have been a survival tool where the environment was not supportive.

Disassociating or disconnecting is the very beginning of the cycle and yet is still a separate stage of the cycle of addiction itself. Disassociation is necessary for the addiction cycle to take place. It can be compared to an airplane traveling down the runway. There is a distinct time that it is on the ground and another distinct time when it has lifted off the runway and is disassociated.

Disassociation is important to understand because it is at this time that we can use behavioral techniques to get grounded. Getting grounded can be as simple as making a phone call or going to a support group. It is while the addict is disassociated, and not yet in the addiction cycle, that he may still have enough sanity to keep the plane on the ground before it takes off to the next level, which would be the beginning of the cycle of addiction. This is crucial for the sex addict to understand so that he can be aware when he is checking out and is not totally available.

Many partners or spouses of sex addicts may complain, "You aren't listening to me," or "You are not here with me, where did you go?" Friends and family of the addict are usually aware when the addict is disassociating or disconnecting and not really listening. This is a common experience for the family of a sex addict. The spouse of a sex addict may often feel kept at a distance.

Disassociation is the stage after the feelings of past or present pain have been felt. The addict needs to do something with his pain and so he disassociates. Then he enters into the beginning of the cycle of addiction.

III. The Altered State (Fantasy World)

Another clinical term we use for trauma survivors and addicts is the altered state. Moving into the altered state is what the recovery community calls "the bubble." The bubble, or the altered state, is a place the addict may have created during his childhood or adolescence that he identified as a safe place. Some people even have names for the place they go although many addicts are not as sophisticated as this, and the altered state is simply a place to "check out" or fantasize. It is a place where the addict creates images or behaviors that may be sexual in nature.

The altered state can be very appealing and soothing. It is an emotional oasis that the sex addict may have created thousands of times. It can include pornography or fantasy about other people, even though they may not actually have had any affairs. We can describe it as the place the sex addict goes to as he looks at others as he walks in the mall. Just as a computer scans a picture into its file, the sex addict may take the picture of the person he scanned and place it in his computer file in his mind to use later to fantasize during his altered state.

The altered state is where the addict goes when he closes his eyes. It is similar to the analogy of the plane. The addict has his pain agent, the plane is on the ground, then he decides it is too painful to handle on his own. So the plane takes off and begins a climb to a cruising altitude. The addict enters the altered state when he reaches the cruising altitude and the plane levels off. He is now in a different reality. In this reality, he is in total control. He can control every image and person in his altered state. He can control other individuals' speech, no matter how degrading or nurturing it is. He can create unlimited possibilities. In this fantasy world of an altered state, the sex addict is all-powerful, all-knowing, in control, loved, cared for and significant. The altered state or nirvana is where the addict has disconnected and checked out. This is a very important part of the sexual addiction cycle. Once the addict has entered the altered state, if he doesn't make phone calls to someone he can be accountable to or pierce "the bubble" somehow by getting back into reality, he will move into the next level of the cycle of addiction.

IV. Pursuing Behavior

Once the addict has achieved the level of the altered state that he created in the bubble, he will now head toward a destination. He may have sophisticated or unsophisticated ways of doing this. Nonetheless, a behavior will be pursued. The pursuit of behavior can be very complicated. The addict has specific repetitious behaviors and once he enters the altered state, he is going to pursue a behavior and act out in some way. It may be pursued alone, with others or in fantasy. The sex addict is in pursuit, much like a plane going to its destination. He has gone from reality to fantasy, and now he is going to create whatever his altered state wants. The sex addict is trying to satiate something that is insatiable, and he has experienced this many times.

During the pursuit, some addicts have specific places they go, people they see, phone calls they make, but whatever is their place, they are in pursuit of a repetitious behavior. For some it may be a very clearly identified location. Some addicts have described it like this, "Yes, I was on my way to a particular place, and was totally out of control. I couldn't feel myself touching the ground at all." At this point, the addict has experienced all the physiological symptoms of being in the altered state and has pursued the behavior.

Pursuing the behavior is a very difficult stage to break unless you have the support of someone who can help you somehow pierce the bubble and get you back into reality.

IV. Behavior

The behavior for sexual addicts can range from being sexual with themselves, voyeurism, pornography, being sexual with others and can include criminal behaviors. The behavior with each sexual addict is different, but the experience is the same. Once the sexual addict goes through the stage where they pursue a behavior, they continue by acting out sexually. The addict compares their sexuality to whatever their altered state is at this time and repeats this behavior over and over again. Every time that they go through this cycle and act out, they reinforce neurologically and psychologically that the addiction is going to medicate their inner being. The reinforcement of this repetitive behavior is their way of dealing with pain and getting through stressors. This final behavior completes the cycle of addiction. This is where they "act out" as they say in Twelve Step groups. This sexual release combined with the altered state reinforces sexual addiction. Those who are in support groups and continue to act out in one way or another won't get better and their lives won't change, if they continue to act out sexually in any way within this cycle. They will basically continue to stay addicts. The best and only way you can stay clean is if you don't reinforce the sexual addiction cycle. This "acting out" behavior completes the cycle of addiction except for one other item--time.

V. Time

I have counseled many sex addicts from various cultural and so-cioeconomic backgrounds and there appears to be an individual pattern for each person. But each person has a definite pattern--and knowing your pattern is key to your recovery.

Some addicts have sexual acting out binges. Others' acting out behaviors are further apart. For most though, there seems to be a set time for the recurrence of pain and the actual acting out behavior. The time between one act and another may be hours, days, weeks or months. There is time between one pain agent and another pain agent. Between these times, if the addict can incorporate their support groups, phone calls and recovery, they can strengthen themselves so that when the next pain agent comes, they can cope with it--rather than giving himself permission to act out because of the pain.

Time is a tricky issue. But between behaviors is your best opportunity to cope before the cycle starts. Pain will come into your life, and you can't control that. But what you can control is what you do with your time, so that when the emotional discomfort, unresolved conflict or need to connect comes along, you can have the strength to say "no" and do something healthy with it instead. As an addict, you need to feel the pain and stay in reality. Find positive behaviors to reinforce that you have value and are worth recovery. You and your family are worth recovery so that you can live a full life physically, emotionally and spiritually. Time can become your best friend. The longer between your last acting out behavior, at any level, the better your life can become. Without support, time can be the only thing that keeps you from your next acting out experience. I would encourage you to memorize your own patterns of pain, disconnecting, altered state and pursuing behavior.

I have observed this cycle of sexual addiction in many addicts over and over again. This cycle is based upon new findings and research since the first cycle was published several years ago. My encouragement is to identify where you are and to move on in the time you have today to recover.

PART TWO
ASPECTS TO
FREEDOM

FIVE COMMANDMENTS TO FREEDOM

5

An Early Plan For Recovery

There are some basic principles that can help sustain your successful recovery from sexual addiction. Early recovery is not simply understanding the facts, nor is it simply talking about sexual addiction. Recovery goes much deeper than talking about what was done In the past.

Let's discuss what I call The Five Commandments to Freedom. These five commandments are simple and can be used much like a checklist that you would put on a wall or mirror at home, where you can see it all the time. You may want to write the commandments down and check off when you have completed them. This is an ideal behavioral checklist for the recovering sexual addict. It assures them that they are putting behavior toward recovery, rather than just coming to an understanding about sexual addiction.

Coming to an understanding is not the only answer for the addict. They may have been in pain for years before and possibly repeated some behaviors hundreds of times. It is for this reason that The Five Commandments, when put in place, give the addict an action plan, so they can begin to arrest the addiction they have been struggling with for so long.

Commandment #1 - Morning Prayer

Prayer is something that many sexual addicts find difficult to do, especially if they have been avoiding spirituality because of the shame and guilt of their behavior, or possibly because of what was done to them in the past. Prayer is simply a behavior that, when put in place, can change the addict's disposition.

We know from all of the other addictions medical science has studied, that an addiction is basically self will run riot. This expression of addiction simply means "doing your own thing." So the first thing in the morning, put aside time to pray. Don't do your own thing. Do Commandment #1 instead.

Prayer, at this point, does not mean that you have to believe in God. It simply means to pray, and praying is talking. When the old timers in Alcoholics Anonymous went to their meetings, they didn't say, "Well if you believe in God, pray." They said, "Get on your knees and pray."

If you don't believe in God, talk to Him about it. You don't have to pray long. You can say, "God, I don't believe in You, but I'm supposed to pray. I want to recover. Would you help me stay sober today?" From that point on, you can also discuss any issues that you want to talk to Him about. He is able to handle hurt, anger, fear, anxiety or any other feeling or thought that you have kept from Him. Prayer is a way for you to behaviorally change yourself. See it as a positive step in your recovery.

Sexual addiction for many addicts starts early in the day--not necessarily the first thing in the morning, but perhaps during the drive to work. Prayer is preventative. It is a way of acknowledging that you are a sexual addict and are in desperate need of sobriety. Without sobriety, you are on a path of self destruction and you'll probably shatter other lives as well. More than likely those around you have been devastated, either through your anger, depression or acting out behavior. As an addict, you are in a fight every day, especially the first 30 to 90 days of recovery. Remember, the first

30 to 90 days is one of the toughest periods of recovery for the sexual addict. Make sure you pray.

Prayer may or may not make you feel better instantly, but if you begin to apply it to your life, you will begin to reap the benefits. Prayer is one of the many new tools that you will have as a recovering person.

Commandment #2 - Phone Calls

Making a phone call can be the very thing that saves you from an acting out experience today. The first step of the Twelve-Steps talks about the word "we." "We" means that you need someone else in your program to help you. In the past, "I" has been the biggest focus in an addict's world. Before recovery the sex addict was powerless. In being powerless, they couldn't fight sexual addiction alone. The addict needs to involve others in the fight for sobriety. Having someone else involved dissipates the energy that comes against the addict. Sexual addiction cannot be dealt with alone. I have not experienced, nor have I met anyone who has experienced sexual addiction recovery alone and maintained not only abstinence, but a life-style of sobriety. When you are not alone, then you are accountable. A life-style of sobriety is a much greater goal than just being abstinent.

There are several ways to address this commandment of making phone calls. One way is to wait until you get into crisis and then call someone to help you. This method does not work, because if you don't have a relationship already established with anyone, you have essentially set up a barrier that isolates you. To make a phone call and say that you are a sex addict is a big enough task to accomplish--let alone calling someone you haven't established a relationship with and telling them of your plight. It's likely you won't make the call at all.

The best way to utilize Commandment #2 is to make one phone call in the morning to another recovering sex addict. Tell them that you are a recovering sexual addict, and you are not in trouble, but if you get in trouble during the day, you are going to use the phone and call them. By doing this you are checked in with someone. Eventually the phone calls will turn into conversations that develop recovery relationships. We need relationships and part of our resocialization is making phone calls, feeling connected, and getting acceptance right at the beginning of the day. If you can make a phone call early in the morning to someone else in the program, you will find the strength you need to succeed during your day.

Like prayer, the phone is a tool you can use to help yourself grow stronger, especially within the first 30-90 days when your need for other people to help is the greatest. The people you call will benefit just as much, if not more, when you call them. Make a phone call to someone else in recovery every day. Again, this commandment, as well as the others, is something you can put on your checklist each day. You don't need to philosophically agree with this concept or have a good feeling about it to decide if you are going to do it. This behavior is designed to help you get sober today.

Commandment #3 - Reading

Reading recovery material that is specifically related to sexual addiction is important. There are many books on the market you can read. It is very important to read some material every day. It is most beneficial to read in the morning. Addicts need to be reminded of what may be in store for them that day. Sometimes what you read will come to mind in a difficult time. Those recovery thoughts can be the very tool to get you out of that tough situation, by giving you the strength to fight it. It is important to involve your mind in your recovery. Your mind alone will not save you, but it may help you to behave so that you can maintain your abstinent behaviors and not cross the line you have drawn. A list of reading materials can be found in the appendix of this book.

By now you probably have a feeling that your morning routine is going to change. These commandments take five to fifteen minutes. They can make a dramatic change in your day. Remember, no matter what you've believed in the past, you are worth getting the recovery you need so that you can restore yourself, your family and your friends. You are going to learn a lot, not only about yourself, but about recovery in general. By doing so, you can successfully integrate into a life-style of hope.

Commandment #4 - Go To Meetings

In AA there is an old expression that says, "There are three times when you should go to a meeting: when you don't feel like going to a meeting, when you do feel like going to a meeting, and at 8 o'clock." It is not a matter of how you feel about it. It is how you behave about it.

In Twelve Step Meetings there is a "ninety meetings in ninety days" rule. This rule is ideal. I counsel with addicts all over the country, and I know that in most major metropolitan areas, there are meetings almost every day of the week.

Meetings are basically to support you and at the same time giving to others what you have learned through your own personal journey of recovery. Being around other recovering sexual addicts is going to help you. First it is going to give you increased hope as you see other sex addicts have more sobriety. Secondly, you may believe that if they can do it, you can too. You can learn many things from others in recovery that they have learned through their own negative or positive experiences. I want to encourage you to go to as many meetings as possible.

If you don't live in a metropolitan area, and can't get to meetings, it can be more difficult for you when you're in a tough situation. An alternative could be getting together frequently with someone you've met at a meeting. This will give you support and a relationship with someone who can help you. The bottom line is, however, you need to be in as many meetings as possible.

I realize some of you reading this don't live in an area where there are groups. I also know some of you might perceive your social status to be at risk if you walked into a sex addicts meeting. In my office we have several independent counselors who have groups for sex addicts and even for intimacy anorexics.

These groups are work groups. You are expected to follow the five commandments, do work in the Step workbook and 101 Exercise workbook. You are expected to call the other members of your group just like you would if you drove across town to go to a meeting. I have found these groups to be tremendously helpful if you don't have a local group or you travel out of town quite a bit.

These principles were established with Dr. Bob and Bill W. in the founding of Alcoholics Anonymous. For information on their development you can get the video called My Name is Bill W. starring James Garner. You will be encouraged by how these principles have worked for more than 60 years with addicted people worldwide. We can help one another if we can get together. If you isolate yourself, you can't be helped, nor can you help others. Some days you will be the one needing the help, and on other days you'll be used to help other sex addicts, which is a great feeling. That is sobriety. When you give that gift away, it reinforces your own recovery.

Commandment #5 - Pray Again

This may sound like work because it is. You can read Commandment #1 again to be reminded that this is not something you have to like or agree with. It is something you just have to behaviorally do. At the end of the day, if you are sober, pray being thankful for a day of sobriety. Sobriety isn't something you do by yourself, it is something you do with the help of God and others. If there are any other issues from the day you want to talk to God about, you can bring them up at this time. If you don't have a relationship with God, ask Him to deepen your relationship with Him, and to send people to you to bring this about. It is important to end your day in a spiritual place in addition to starting the day this way. The recovery program that is going to work is spiritual in nature. So, it is important to reestablish your own spirituality since you were born a spirit, with a soul, living in a body. While most addicts give attention to their souls (their mind, wills and emotions) and their bodies, they usually don't nurture their spirit component. Make this a time of being thankful that you had a day of sobriety today. Even the worst day in sobriety is something to be thankful for, because even on the best day without recovery, you were covered with shame, guilt and fear. So, if you have any relief from those feelings, I believe it is appropriate to pray.

Tips For Finding a Twelve-Step Group

Unlike other addiction support groups such as Alcoholics Anonymous and Narcotics Anonymous, Sex Addicts Twelve-Step support groups vary. There are several groups to choose from and all over the country they vary from region to region, and within regions as well.

The three major groups for sexual addicts are Sexaholics Anonymous, Sex Addicts Anonymous, and Sex and Love Addicts Anonymous. These three groups make up the majority of sexual addiction Twelve-Step groups. These three groups interface differently in different parts of the country.

In your search for a support group, you can try any of these three Twelve-Step groups. A broad generalization is that Sexaholics Anonymous is generally known to be more like an Alcoholics Anonymous program in which a slip is a slip and is acknowledged as such. In Sex Addicts Anonymous there appears to be more tolerance of behaviors, generally speaking. Sex and Love Addicts Anonymous deals more with the love addiction component regarding chasing relationships and trying to be fixed by people in your life. Because these groups vary even further among themselves, any one group may or may not deal with the sexual compulsive part of the addiction. This is an important distinction. If someone is mostly a sex addict, they need to be in a group that deals specifically with the compulsive behavior of sexually acting out.

My encouragement would be to find the Twelve-Step groups in your area. Pick one that addresses the sexual compulsive behavior. If you are limited to only one group in your area, then you don't have much of an option. I still encourage you to attend. You'll have to work around whatever it is in that particular group that is lacking, but you will still benefit from everything else the group can offer. What you will need from the group as a recovering sex addict is a point of identification with others. Just knowing that others in the support group know what you're dealing with when you say, "You know what I mean?" makes all the difference. They know the pain, shame, guilt and fears you have walked with and can appreciate the courage it takes to be honest. There is a lot more shame and guilt included in this particular addiction compared with other addictions. Any group is going to be better than no group.

Sex addicts need a place to be honest. Honesty is going to be a new skill for those who have mastered being dishonest and have lived two different lives. In your support group, you can begin to practice sharing things that you have never shared before and get a positive response for being honest, especially from people who know what it is taking you to break through.

Encouragement is another thing needed from the group. Encouragement comes in various forms. It may come in the form of one person working their recovery successfully and another person being able to say, "Wow, that's something I want to have." This type of encouragement happens frequently in Twelve-Step support groups. It is encouraging when one addict works on their recovery to the point where it inspires others. There is a lot of work that is to be done in the Twelve-Step groups. When someone does the work, it encourages others to work on their own recovery.

Feedback is crucial for the sexual addict. When the addict is in denial, the addict is unable to feel and connect with the pain they have caused others or even to themselves. Sometimes getting feedback from others can help them get in touch with some of the pain that they have been running from.

Feedback can also help some of the cognitive thinking or what they call in Alcoholics Anonymous "stinking thinking," and get the addict into sober thinking. It can also challenge some behaviors and establish boundaries. The feedback portion of the group will happen at what is called "check in time." After the meeting the leader of the group may say "Does anyone want to check in?" This is when you will share where you really are in your recovery, get honest with two other people, and get feedback if you want it. Other people who have been where you are can help you get through and get what you want in your recovery. Feedback can help quite a bit.

When you attend a Twelve-Step meeting, make sure you get a phone list from the group, if they have one, or approach a couple of people after the meeting and ask them for their phone numbers. Having phone numbers of other recovering sex addicts when you need them is crucial to your personal recovery. Practice making phone calls to other members in the group on a daily basis. This is the safety net for your early recovery. Phone calls can ultimately save you from a future relapse.

Another benefit of your support group is spirituality. As you look at the Twelve-Steps (We'll go over these in Chapter 11), you will notice that God is mentioned quite a bit. Some addicts may not have been able to connect with God, because of the guilt and shame of their own behavior. Some may have had a relationship with God but because of the addiction, they were living incongruent with their relationship to God and now feel distant. In a support group, you will see some people with the same faith, who begin to piece back their relationship with God and begin to see a serenity in living congruently with what they know to be true. You also will see those who listen to their intuition. When they know they are in danger, they won't act out. You will hear about some addicts praying and getting alleviated from a current situation that they needed help with, so that they could stay sober. Spirituality is more often caught than taught. As you go to Twelve-Step meetings, you will begin to catch the flavor of spirituality and add it into your life in such a way that it makes sense. God makes sense when we see someone across the room getting help. We know then that He can probably help us, too. If God can provide the things necessary in the program, then you can probably expect to get some positive results. You will find that God isn't some mystical far away being, but rather quite practical and relational. Through the group, you will receive something that you may not know that you need--unconditional love.

Unconditional love is something we rarely get in our lives and when we do get it, it changes us. Unconditional love is often a part of Twelve-Step groups. The other addicts in the group have been where you are, and they are loved by others that have been there. And now that you are there, you can receive the love that they have for you. When they stand up to give you a hug, it may feel uncomfortable at first, but let it happen and receive the love that they have for you. They know that after you have done your first step, they will know all of your secrets. As one old-timer said, "It sounds like you are one of us." The acceptance and unconditional love you will receive from this group is something you may not have known you needed. It will feel like a weight has been lifted off you when unconditional love comes your way. Many sex addicts have not been loved for who they really are. The group is a place where you can be unconditionally loved because they know you and accept you, just like you are.

Practicing these Five Commandments and attending group meetings can allow you to see others who are reaching the final freedom. If you need to locate a group go to our website www.sexaddict.com and click the link for groups. My hope is that you can give this to yourself and inspire the others who are on the journey to the final freedom.

THE FIVE COMMANDMENTS

Commandment #1 - Morning Prayer
Commandment #2 - Phone Calls
Commandment #3 - Reading
Commandment #4 - Go To Meetings
Commandment #5 - Pray Again

BIOLOGICAL FREEDOM

6

Biological treatment is a very import aspect for most sex addicts. Sex addicts have biological and neurological training and conditioning that went on within their body as well as their brain. In this chapter when I discuss the brain, I am not talking about the thought life of the sex addict, but the gray matter that is between our ears, the actual organ that has its own biological needs, development and conditioning.

Similar to other muscles in your body that can be conditioned, you can condition the brain. We discussed earlier in The Biological Aspects how the brain actually does evolve into a place where the sex addict, through ejaculation in an altered state experience, can become the primary way in which the brain gets its needs met. Therefore it is important to look at the biological treatment of sexual addiction.

This is often an overlooked aspect of the treatment of the sex addict and it is for this reason we placed it first in the treatment of sex addiction. I firmly believe that the body is part of the recovery process. I have witnessed too many sex addicts who did not take their body seriously and relapsed because of their lack of respect for what had been going on with their body and brain for many years before they started treatment. It is for this reason we are going to look at this from what may seem like a detached perspective. We need to look at what happened to our brain while in the midst of the addiction.

In our addiction, we conditioned our body and our sexuality to certain stimuli such as pornography or fantasy and ejaculated while in that state. Let's look at the conditioning process. The sex addict goes into a fantasy and he starts "cooking" it. This is the cue from a conditioning process that we will label "A."

"A" will lead to the addiction cycle and pursue the behavior. The behaviors we'll call "B" will send "C" (the endorphins and enkephalin) to the brain. In our brain there is very little distinction between "A" and "C". The brain, as an organ, notes that the addict is starting to cook something and knows what behaviors are going to follow and that "C" is going to happen next. This is the simple process in which the sex addict conditioned himself.

The sex addict is unaware of this conditioning and that it feeds off itself and becomes stronger and stronger with repetition. It is important to look at this conditioning since it is so powerful. Anyone who is married knows that conditioning is powerful. If every time you took out the garbage you got a kiss, you would never have to be told to take it out. It would be a conditioned response. We are creatures of conditioning and this can be worked to our advantage or disadvantage. In addiction, it works toward our detriment. In recovery it can work toward our benefit.

How can we recondition ourselves as it relates to our sex addiction? The reconditioning process will work similarly in the fashion of A to B to C. When we start having sexually inappropriate thoughts, and for newly recovering sex addicts this will be frequently, we can put a rubber band around our wrist. Every time we have an inappropriate thought we snap the rubber band on the inside of our wrist. This exercise goes into greater detail in 101 Practical Exercises for Sexual Addiction Recovery, along with many other exercises that help in the reconditioning process. When we snap the rubber band, "P" will happen, which stands for pain. It will take about 30 days for this process to take the reconditioning effect. Some say a positive thought, after they snap the rubber band. Neurologically, when you get an inappropriate thought, your body is going to start associating it with pain. Most clients report to me that within a month of this reconditioning behavior, 80 percent of their sexual inappropriate thought life disappears. At this point most are ecstatic!

This fantasy life has been a part-time job for most sex addicts. Now they have just increased their productivity about 15-20 hours a week! It is enjoyable to have your thoughts under control and not have your time taken away by your fantasies. Reconditioning is vital for sexual addiction treatment. This is just one aspect.

Another aspect, from a biological perspective, is accountability. Accountability with your time, money, thoughts, and sexual behaviors is crucial. Finding someone to be accountable to brings into play a very important behavioral conditioning. When I was working on my master's degree, I started to work on my sexual addiction recovery. At that time I had no idea that it was an addiction, I just knew it was a problem. I made myself accountable to someone. I told them that if I acted out in any particular way, I would be honest with them and tell them. In the beginning, I was successful so it was not a problem. Then I relapsed. The pain involved in telling this person that I slipped was so terrific that it made me less likely to want to do it again. The pain of telling someone that you acted out is far greater than the pleasure of acting out. After that first experience, if I was alone and had inappropriate thoughts beginning, I jumped out of bed and went to the gym or did something so that I would not act out again, because I could not stand the pain of telling someone that I had acted out. For this purpose it is important not to have your wife be the person you are accountable to. It is important to be accountable to someone of the same sex. This accountability sets up a reconditioning experience. It is not an experience you want to repeat again and again. Eventually this accountability will set up a conditioning so that you can experience a reconditioning aspect to your sex addiction.

Many sex addicts have rationalizations that they use to behave in the way that they do sexually. For example, "My life is a mess, I deserve it," or "I'm so stressed out." These rationalizations can lead the sex addict back into his behavior.

To recondition this behavior you can write a letter about how you feel after you act out. Include in it your feelings of guilt, loneliness, despair, or hopelessness and the pain that you feel. Pick the worst situation and include it in this letter. Now say aloud one of the thoughts that pulls you into your acting out behavior. For example: "Just one more time, then I'll stop." After you say this, read the letter. Repeat this two times, twice a day for about a week. This will do the exact opposite of what your addiction has done. In your addiction you have conditioned your thoughts "Just one more time" to equal acting out. This was conditioned. Now after this exercise you have taken the same process and used it for your benefit. You begin to connect with those words to pain. You will begin to associate this thought process with discomfort. Being the creatures that we are, we try to avoid pain, therefore, this will work for your benefit.

As we discussed in the chapter on biological aspects of sex addiction, some people may be depressed. Their brain, for whatever reason, does not produce enough endorphins or enkephalins to make them feel normal. The addict therefore has learned to modify their neurological balance through the burst of endorphins and enkephalins when they act out, which makes them feel normal. This may be the only time they feel this way. Once the person who is biologically depressed gets into recovery, he may move into a deep depression characterized by not sleeping, sleeping all the time, not eating, eating constantly, energy loss, feeling worthless or hopeless or maybe even having suicidal thoughts. This is not the norm, but it does happen to some sex addicts beginning in recovery. This tells me that there is a biological depression that preceded the addiction and has been one of the major agents why the sex addict is in his addiction. Unfortunately, because of the unhealthy solution that he chose to fix his brain's chemical imbalance, the addict needs now to recover just the same as any other sex addict. He still needs to work The Five Commandments, and be accountable. Taking medicine will not cure the defects in the developmental dwarfing because of the addiction. A biological depression is going to need a biological solution. The biological solutions available today far exceed anything we have known so far in the history of medicine. There are many antidepressants that psychiatrists recommend. The biological depression will not get better with spiritual or psychological application. If you had a bullet wound, you need a doctor to take care of it. The sex addict who is biologically depressed needs not only the recovery steps we've discussed thus far, but also a biological solution such as antidepressants and the care of a physician.

PSYCHOLOGICAL FREEDOM

There are several goals to keep in mind in the psychological freedom of a sex addict. In this chapter, we will discuss some of the major aspects of the psychological healing process. The first of the psychological processes deals with the psychological dependency in sex addiction. As discussed earlier, the addict often becomes psychologically dependent on his addiction. I sometimes address this as "the first wife." This is the first place the sex addict discovered in his developmental life that he could have his needs met.

Psychological Dependency

Another exercise from 101 Practical Exercise for Sexual Addiction Recovery crystallizes what a sex addict gets out of his addiction from a psychological aspect. Here's the exercise: Write a thank you letter and a good-bye letter to your sex addiction. The sex addict needs to look at what the addiction has done for him. It has often kept him from being responsible or intimate in relationships, justified his leaving relationships, kept him feeling powerful, loving, always in control, and successful in his addiction. In your letter, thank your sexual addiction for what it has done for you from your adolescence, early adulthood, all the way through to the present. This will give you a good idea of the psychological dependence you have on your addiction in the past.

The next step is to write a good-bye letter. This will give you a point and time of when you confront the psychological dependence. This has actually been a relationship that you have had. It has been a real person you have clung to in your fantasy world. Some have even crystallized this person specifically. It is now important to face the psychological dependence of the sex addiction so that you can also confront the issues. From this letter you may be able to deduce some of the other issues that you need to deal with as far as the psychological dependence. If the dependence was for escape or entertainment, you are going to need to look at those issues and make a plan for legitimately meeting those needs in another way. We do need to have fun, entertainment, and be loved in a healthy way. Sex addiction was there often times to compensate for those needs not being met. In recovery, it will be your responsibility to identify these needs and find a healthy process of meeting them. The first aspect is to deal with the psychological dependency. This letter will be a beginning for this and again you can refer to 101 Practical Exercises for Sex Addiction Recovery for further details.

Family of Origin

For many addicts, the family of origin is a complicated issue. A majority of addicts grew up in homes that were dysfunctional. And they may have been dysfunctional in many different ways. Their family could have been neglectful to where they weren't praised or celebrated or invested in. Another way their family may have been dysfunctional is that there were other addictions in the family such as food, nicotine, work or sex which would make the environment that the sex addict grew up in very distant and emotionally absent.

Children from this kind of environment grow up to be without skills to deal with life's stresses or issues. The child is then left to decide which addiction they will choose to medicate the absence of those skills and/or the pain of the distance within the family. There is also the more abusive, angry or volatile family system that can produce an addictive person. Abandonments could be in the addict's family of origin including divorces where one of the parents leave. The child is then susceptible to psychological pain, which is one of the pain agents for addiction.

As you look at your family of origin, you may find causes for issues you are dealing with. How did your parents deal with anger? Did they show love? In this chapter we are just highlighting the psychological aspects that need to be addressed during treatment. Individual therapy may be needed while looking at these issues. If there is a lot of pent up anger which can show up in either the form of depression or hostility toward either mom or dad, this will need to be addressed in your treatment. Anger is held within your body and keeps you in pain. From the psychological aspect, to recover from sex addiction, you will have to heal your mind, will and emotions that are hurting because of neglect, abuse or dysfunctionalism in your family of origin. If this is a large issue for yourself, seek qualified professional help.

On the other hand, some sex addicts grew up in an ideal situation. They are biological sex addicts who don't have family of origin issues to deal with. But they will still need to do quite a bit of work, but not in this particular area.

Feelings

This is a major part of sexual addiction recovery. During our development years, many of us did not learn to identify or communicate feelings, and yet feelings can be one of the most treacherous and dangerous areas in our early recovery. Many sex addicts have at some point felt unloved, rejected or unappreciated, which puts them into a difficult place if they don't know how to express their feelings. Many addicts end up medicating through a unhealthy sexual activity as a way of dealing with feelings. In any addiction, I find that feelings are something that addicts don't have much skill in fully expressing. This is just a lack of a particular skill issue. It is not a matter of a level of intelligence.

In the midst of the addiction, when the sex addict had a feeling, and didn't know what it was, when they acted out, it went away. It was a simple solution. But in recovery, they don't have the solution of acting out. Now they have the problem of having a feeling and not knowing what it is.

The following is an exercise that can help facilitate this. It is called the Feeling Exercise.

1. I feel _____ when _____.
2. I first remember feeling _____ when _____.

This exercise is difficult at first. It's like learning a new computer program. Although it may be frustrating at first, eventually you will get familiar with it and then wonder how you lived without it. First we identify the feeling. Without doing this part of the exercise, you can't do the second part, which is communicate. In the appendix, you will find a feelings list. Pick a feeling word from the list and fill in the blanks.

For example:

1. I feel calm when I go to the lake with my friend.
2. I first remember feeling calm when I was playing with an electric train set my mother bought me.

In this example I am giving a picture. These are to be very specific experiences. What we are doing is creating files. Our emotions as sex addicts are similar to a messy desk. We are taking the papers off the desk in this exercise and putting them in a filing system that goes a, b, c, d,... In computer language, it's like having a data base without file names on the data base. If we look for a file, we can't find it. This makes the addict feel like he doesn't know what to do, think or feel, and so he acts out. Being able to identify feelings is very important. Do this exercise daily for about a month so that your verbal language increases. Write them down and you will be able to experience some feelings. After your first 30 days of abstinence, you are going to find yourself having some feelings. It is important to realize what you are feeling so that you don't relapse.

The second part of this feeling exercise is communication. You can do this exercise with a therapist or with someone in your recovery group. You will need to communicate the feeling sentences that you have completed. I encourage you not to do this over the phone. Some may want to do this exercise with their partner or spouse. It is important if you do this with your partner or spouse, that you do NOT use your relationship in any way shape or form as examples. An example of what NOT to do:

I feel frustrated when you don't pick up your socks. You can feel frustrated when you drive down the highway or when the dog sleeps in your favorite chair, but don't aim it at your partner, and don't use the word "you." The way I first explained this is the only way this exercise should be done with your partner, otherwise it will lead to another way to battle each other.

If this exercise is done correctly, it can provide a safe place for you to communicate your feelings. While one person is sharing their feelings, the other one can listen. The person listening shouldn't make comments on the feelings shared for 72 hours. This creates a security for both to know that they are safe to communicate their feelings. This exercise will accelerate moving you from feeling frozen to thawed. This exercise will be like sitting in the microwave emotionally. Without this exercise, I find that the sex addict seems to have more relapses, and it also takes a lot longer period of time to develop intimacy, which we will discuss next.

Intimacy

Most spouses want intimacy with their sexually addicted partners, but sex addicts have no idea what their partners are talking about. In early recovery, the addict was unable to become intimate because their feelings were still frozen and they didn't have the skills necessary to be intimate. Intimacy is the result of having the skills and emotions. Because the addict has been medicating their emotions for so long, they are underdeveloped. The addict is really unable to develop the kind of intimacy that a lot of people experience and what their spouse may want from them. If you are in recovery, intimacy is an obtainable goal for your future.

Intimacy is basically the ability to be able to share your heart, feelings, or the deeper part of yourself with another human being. You will sense feelings of acceptance and love mutually. It has sort of a spiritual aspect to it. You will feel connected, close and warm. Sex addicts, in their development, have learned not to share with people because of a lie they believe: "If you knew me, you wouldn't love me." Consequently, many sex addicts have not experienced intimacy and, therefore, don't believe it exists. They need to grow past this. You can practice intimacy and get better at it. This takes months, but as you practice sharing and being honest, you will experience intimacy. You'll begin to add to your experiences and the more experiences you have, the more you will believe and accept the existence of intimacy. This is an integral part of the final freedom.

Trauma

Trauma is common to most sex addicts. It may have been emotional, spiritual, physical, or sexual abuse and/or neglect. Trauma comes in many shapes, sizes and forms. It is a very important piece in your psychological recovery. In this book we are unable to go into great detail about trauma, since it could be a whole book unto itself.

Being a victim of trauma, abandonment and neglect, I have had to work through trauma personally and it has been healing to do so. After about 45 days clean in recovery, I find my clients are ready to work on their trauma issues. You will need to have your feelings in place before you can deal with trauma.

There are techniques you can use to address trauma. First identify what your trauma was. As you go through your feelings, you may go through some recall of what has been traumatizing to you. As a person whose feelings are frozen, you may not realize what actually was trauma, but as you thaw out in your recovery, trauma may become more obvious to you. As you complete Steps Four and

Five, you will find more information that will lead you to believe there has been trauma in your life.

When you identify the trauma, make a list of the incidents so that you know what you are going to be dealing with. You will need a competent professional to help you through your trauma issues. You may want to read the section on how to find a therapist for this work. There are cognitive exercises as well as writing exercises to work through the trauma.

I believe if you deal with trauma early in your recovery, you will be more successful in your recovery. Trauma work is essential for successful sex addiction recovery. Without it, you keep the psychological pain. With that pain, you keep the drive to medicate within you. This is not what you need to do to yourself. You are worth recovery, and having the best life possible. But you will need to open up the secrets you have kept inside. If you have secrets, it may be that they are trauma secrets. Secrets can keep you sick and in your addiction. If you are keeping a trauma secret, it is important that you get honest. Many sex addicts have been sexually abused by older women or men, and don't call it sexual abuse. I have had clients who could not acknowledge it as abuse, and they ended up expanding the length of their recovery considerably. Once you have identified these traumas, you will want to begin working on them.

You are worth recovery! It may be hard work at times to peel through some of the layers you might have but you are worth the final freedom.

SPIRITUAL FREEDOM

8

Spirituality is a crucial element in the sex addict's recovery. The human being is spiritual and that part of the human must be nurtured. The spirituality of the sex addict may not have been nurtured or experienced during his growing up years. Sexual addiction robs the sex addict of emotional, relational, vocational, and sometimes of social and spiritual development. For some sex addicts, spirituality is a new concept.

Spirituality has minimally two very large facets. The first is the spiritualness of just being human. This is our natural ability to be honest, open-minded and able to hear and connect with others in a spiritual sense. By learning to nurture these traits, our intuition can grow back into place. Intuition is the inner part of ourselves where we sense something without having all the information. We recognize something by the feeling or the sense of it. When we violate this "inner voice," we tend to pay heavy consequences.

My intuition has become very crucial in my recovery. It tells me when I am around safe or unsafe people. This intuition is part of my spiritual recovery, which has been a great gift to me. Over time in recovery you need to nurture and develop that voice so that you can hear your spirit--your inner self--talking to you. Spiritual recovery is a dynamic experience, especially in Twelve Step groups where we are honest with each other and have a sense of empathy and compassion, a sense of genuine willingness to encourage another addict. Spirituality is living in congruence with ourselves.

Spirituality is also the part of us that relates to "a power greater than ourselves." Note that it does not state "a higher power" in the Twelve-Steps; it says a greater power than ourselves. This is a single power that is greater than all of us. This is not a human power. Those who are past Step Two have come to the concept of having a relationship with God.

Coming into a relationship with God can be a scary thing for some sex addicts. Many have run away from God or have compartmentalized Him to only one part of their lives. Others with religious backgrounds may have God in a box and bring Him out on Sunday and Wednesday nights. God wasn't in the sex addict's sexuality, finances, or relationships, nor was the sex addict able to be intimate with God.

Spirituality came to me in a nonreligious experience with the Lord Jesus Christ. This relationship has become a whole person relationship over the period of my recovery, which has been essential to my sobriety. Many others find this essential also in their recovery. I have worked with many sex addicts who start off from scratch having had no spiritual background whatsoever. Some are antagonistic toward God and have been avoiding Him through their addiction. Others have felt too ashamed to believe that God would ever love or accept them again. To those I would only say, stay with your recovery long enough to enjoy the spiritual recovery. Opening up yourself to God, no matter what your belief system is, can start as simply as following the first of The Five Commandments, praying in the morning by asking God to keep you clean today. If this is all you can begin to verbalize to God, that is a great start.

Believing in God is not a prerequisite to praying. Many people have grown and nurtured their spiritual beings simply by behaving in spiritual ways, by praying. Even agnostics and atheists can come into a spiritual belief system about God in their recovery, marriage, or in their business, which sometimes triples in the first year of recovery. I have seen this and this is exciting for the sex addict.

Spirituality has application in all of our lives. The beginning of nurturing this would be to simply have prayer. If you are past Step Two or Three, this has become a daily part of your life. I encourage recovering sex addicts, no matter what stage they are in, to keep prayer as part of their personal growth. It is a way to meet that inner need. The sponge inside needs to be watered. Spirituality is a great way to nurture the human being.

Spirituality is a developmental process. This development may be building upon something you have already known and experienced, or you may be building from scratch. Those of you who are building from scratch, I encourage you to pray and listen to the experience, hope and strength of others in your Twelve Step meetings. Examine the lives of those experiencing good recovery. Investigate their spiritual belief system and incorporate what is good for you. Some have come from Jewish, Protestant and Catholic backgrounds. Being raised in the church can be a very positive experience in recovery, just like being raised in a healthy family is great. Some of us have experienced dysfunctional church systems. Some have experienced spirituality in a very negative and shaming light during their growing up years. But this doesn't mean that all the churches are unspiritual or even unhealthy.

If you've grown up in a church or synagogue, building on whatever you have experienced in the past will be helpful. At some point in your recovery, investigate this belief and your walk with God. In my belief system, coming back to Jesus Christ was imperative in my recovery. Without that returning, I would not have become whole in my recovery.

My encouragement is to experience spirituality by behaving spiritually. Surround yourself with people who are growing spiritually. If you intend to grow spiritually, you are going to need to be around people who value spirituality. You can't measure spirituality, nor put a price tag on it, and you need to be around those who have this disposition in life, who believe spirituality is important.

Spirituality can be delicious to the human being because it completes him. There is something very positive about having no shame before God and being able to be thankful, which is an indication in recovery that a person is growing spiritually. A recovering addict will begin to be thankful that he was chosen out of the many who die from this disease to become whole. He will become thankful that he is being restored to himself and to his family--and to the generations to come. Spirituality is a generational blessing once we open the door.

9

GOOD GRIEF

Grief is a natural process which human beings work through to naturally move through pain. One painful reality could be the death of a loved one. The pain of that loss is often overwhelming so the process of grief allows us to take pain in increments or stages. We will cover the stages, but first we will discuss how sex addicts grieve. Sex addicts go through the grieving process at several levels and over several different issues.

As the sex addict recovers, he grieves over his sexual addiction. I would like to express sexual addiction as a multifaceted relationship. It is a biological relationship. Often our sexual addiction has been there all our lives. It has been there to run to and nurture us, and it has been our primary route to false intimacy. It has been with some sex addicts 10 to 50 years, and often was the first sexual experience.

So sexual addiction is often a loss of a relationship that you can no longer have. It is the loss of a best friend for many sex addicts. Losing your best friend can be painful. In all honesty, all of our relationships outside of recovery are usually secondary relationships. The secret life was primary. When you count up the hours the sex addict spent in their sexual addiction, you find that sex addiction has absorbed thousands of hours of time. So to say good bye to a friend, who has been there all the time, every time, is difficult. Non-addicts or co-addicts will not understand this relationship, just like others don't understand what it is like to lose a parent unless they have gone through it themselves.

In going through this grief of losing a primary relationship, you may not meet people who understand, unless they are people in your Twelve Step group who have also gone through the grief and loss of a significant relationship. Your new life without addiction can be very scary. Grief is a way to avoid this change and growth. It is a way to help us experience the pain of our loss and move through. By moving through it successfully, we can enjoy the rest of our lives with other primary relationships, such as our partners and children.

The Loss of Our Image

Our image is what we present to the world. For sex addicts that is about 90 percent of our lives. We project an image of sometimes being very competent, strong, intelligent, successful, and often almost perfect. A sex addict I had in treatment once said that when he came into recovery, one of the things his wife said to him was, "How am I going to accept you as being imperfect? I'm used to relating to you as being perfect." Often there is over compensation for being an addict. We feel we have to be more than human, so we project this image to our peers, co-workers, family, and friends. It is a way that many sex addicts use to cope and hide their sexual addiction. Losing an image that we have crafted and perfected is quite a large loss. It is the loss of self as defined by our addiction. This loss of self can be just as large as the loss of addiction. It is the loss of who I am to the outside world and now I am redefining that through recovery. It is similar to what children go through with their parents. When they are young they think that their parents are wonderful, but when they get older they think they are terrible. Then as an adult they realize that their parents were just people. These are the kind of phases we are going to be going through ourselves. Just realizing that developmentally we are human beings means realizing that we have flaws and strengths. We don't have to pretend. We can relax and "be," instead of trying to perform an image for others and base our acceptance on this performance.

The loss of image to ourselves is significant, and there also may be reciprocal grief as far as the loss of our image to others because they also depended on our image for their own purposes.

The Loss of People

As sex addicts, we may have related to other partners outside of our primary relationship. The losses of some of these relationships can be very painful. Indeed, we have over idealized our sexual relationships, and in our early recovery, it was very difficult to separate the fact that our relationship was based on sex. The loss of places that we may have gone to is also a part of the loss where we may have received social reinforcement in our previous acting out days. These are losses we are going to incur early in our sexual addiction recovery only because we have depended upon these structures and our addiction to survive. I use the term "survive" and not live, because a sexual addict has only just begun to live as he enters recovery. In a lot of ways he has only experienced a limited amount of what life has to offer, and now that he is in recovery, he has to go through the grief process and let it give him a new life.

Grief Stages

The stages of grief have been outlined by Koogler Ross as she worked with those who were dying of cancer. These stages have been applied to many aspects of life such as losing loved ones to death, divorce or injury. Loss of a primary relationship, such as what a sex addict has with his addiction, is important to discuss.

Stage One - Shock

Shock is a feeling you experience when you are initially confronted with a painful reality, such as acknowledging you are a sex addict. The first time it was mentioned to you, for a moment, you may have felt a realization of "What am I doing?" That was shock. Shock is a feeling that is beyond communication, but you know when you have experienced it. I have seen many sex addicts experience this stage in my office as they discover the truth about their addiction.

Stage Two - Denial

To deny something means you have a "knowing" on some level that it is true. You can't deny something unless you know that there is some validity to it. So denial is a defense mechanism which allows us not to see or feel or connect with the truth of what is real. For example, if someone died, we might say they are not dead. In this case, we would hope that denial would not last for a long time. Unfortunately in the case of addiction, denials can last for years, and in some situations can lead a person to death.

Denial is so great in sexual addiction it can kill. Sex addicts, who are acting out in populations that are high risk for AIDS, simply say there is nothing wrong with it, and that they are not going to get AIDS. This is a defense mechanism which allows them to maintain their addiction.

Many sex addicts have numerous ways of denying their addiction before they come into an acceptance of being a sex addict. Some denial statements are "everybody does it," "I didn't lose my job," or "I'm not hurting anybody." Denial is a great way of saying I'm not what I know that I am. This can be contagious in a family system where everyone agrees that you are a wonderful person and so there is no one to confront your denial.

Denial is usually broken by two methods. One method is the pain inside becomes so great that you experience the reality that you are a sex addict. Another method can be experienced by getting arrested or being threatened by divorce, or getting caught in an act of your addiction.

Denial is a phase that everyone goes through. The Twelve-Steps help a recovering addict stay out of denial. Having people who love us enough to see our denial is important for a sex addict. If denial has been an issue for you, in your more rational moments, express the kind of denial statements that you have to your support team, such as your sponsor, group members, or spouse, so they can reiterate it to you during your denial. Denial is tricky, and when you reenter it, it will lead you to a path of destruction back into your addiction.

I have seen some addicts decide that they are not really addicts, only to finally realize that they are. Some have incurred serious consequences from going back into the addiction. My encouragement is that if you are in denial about any part of your addiction; share what you are thinking with others who are serious about recovery. Believe what other people are seeing more than what you are saying.

Stage Three - Anger

Anger is a good stage of grief. This means that we are finally interacting with the painful truth. We don't like pain. It is uncomfortable and we are mad. We are mad that sometimes life has chosen to give us a limitation. We are mad that we can't act out the way we used to or be with the people we were within the past. We are mad that a disease such as sex addiction is cut out of our life. We are mad that God has chosen to heal us. All of these things are a part of anger and grief. As a recovering person myself, I wondered why others could have sugar and caffeine when I couldn't. Being angry about this is normal and shows that we are making progress. It is not a sign that we are going backward. Eventually the anger will go away, or at least not be as prevalent, as you go through the stages of grief. If you feel like there is a need to grapple with the anger, you can write your addiction a letter of what it has done to you over the years. This will help you work through your feelings. You can write about how your addiction has kept you from intimacy, honesty, enjoying life and productivity. Anger will also come up if you are a survivor of abuse, which may have been a factor in you becoming a sex addict. Anger shows that you are connecting with feelings. If you find that you need further help with your anger, consult a therapist and discuss techniques you can use to deal with your anger, so that you can move to the next stage. Anger is important to manage for you to maintain recovery.

Stage Four - Bargaining

Bargaining is a stage of grief that involves an "if...then" logic. For example, "If something wouldn't have been in my past, then I wouldn't have become a sex addict," or "If I could stop doing this for 30 days, I wouldn't be a sex addict." The bargaining can go on and on. It is an attempt to try to shift the pain and manipulate it to fit into categories and still not experience the full impact of it. There is no shame in going through bargaining as long as you know that you are bargaining with your addiction.

As long as you are going to your Twelve-Step meetings and keeping The Five Commandments you are probably going to be okay. Allow some caring people to be aware of your statements and confront you when they hear them so that you can continue to move into acceptance. Being what you are is the most freeing experience you will ever have. Our limitations are there so that we cannot destroy our lives. Coming to that recognition is a part of grief. This again is a normal process.

Stage Five - Sadness

For the sex addict, sadness is going to hit when he has been sober over a period of time and is not just attending meetings. When he starts having feelings, one of the feelings he will experience is sadness. This sadness may be over the things lost because of addiction, and because of the damages he may have caused and the risks that were taken. Some will think that they are perhaps going into depression. It can and it may affect you this way. Your eating, sleeping and energy level may be disturbed. If this goes on for a long time, you will need to consult a therapist about it, but it is normal to go through this stage. You will find some periods of crying unrelated to any significant event. You will feel vulnerable at times. You may find you are isolating yourself from others. It is sad that we have developed and behaved the way we did. And yet to recover, hope is just one more stage away. Experience the feeling of sadness and understand that it is okay to feel this way because you are close to the end of your grief process. There is no way of getting through the grief process without feeling this emotion of sadness.

Stage Six - Acceptance

Acceptance is more than an intellectual or philosophical agreement that something is true. Acceptance is integration that something is true. I can cognitively know that someone is dead, but integrating that and behaving as if it were true is a clear indicator that I have come to acceptance. In the case of a sex addict, it is someone who is behaving as if what he knows to be true is true. He is going to meetings, making phone calls, has motivation toward recovery, and finds creative solutions not to act out. It is an awareness that he is what God has allowed him to be created as, with a limitation in the area of sex, and is willing to take responsibility for this. Part of showing that this is what I am is behavioral. I will behave as if I am a recovering sex addict and will find the greatest freedom in behaving as who I am, as opposed to trying to create an image or system to cover up what I am. In acceptance, I will accept my addiction and other painful events that have happened in my life.

Embracing Grief

Grief is something you will go through in various levels and various times, and so it is important that we look at how we grieve. One way to grieve is resistant. Resistant grief is when we push against the process. We don't want to feel the pain. We aren't praying and asking for help grieving or feel the pain. But the more we resist, the longer it is going to take. Grief has no agenda of its own. It doesn't necessarily take one or two years. It is the disposition that we take with grief that determines how long it takes to go through the process. We can embrace grief and let it take us through the process of healing, or we can resist it and just let it stand by our side until we embrace it.

Embracing grief is coming to a place of knowing that recovery is a process and that you are going through these stages and embrace them. If you are reading this book, you are probably already out of shock and probably working toward moving out of denial and possibly further. You are to already be congratulated and yet there are more stages ahead of you. The new life of intimacy is just ahead of you, so be encouraged. If you can embrace the process, you can expedite it to a certain degree.

Grief and Our Partner

Sex addicts are not the only ones, of course, who go through grief. The addiction is not only a painful reality to the addict, but it is a painful reality to the partner and family of the sex addict as well. In looking at partners, the grief process for them is different than the grief process for the addict. When the addict finds out he is a sex addict and breaks through denial, he usually has a sense of relief that this is what he is. This is known as the "pink cloud syndrome" and it can last anywhere from four to six weeks in which the addict feels so good that he has finally identified that he is a sex addict. During this time, the addict may not understand his partner's grief.

The partner is experiencing some painful realities, such as limitations of being married to a sexual addict, possible infidelity or a risk of health. The partner of the addict is going through a lot of pain. The loss of who she thought her spouse was and who he actually is can sometimes be so diametrically opposed that she may have to go through grief to even begin to integrate all these realizations. When the partner finds out about the sex addiction, she is not going to go through a long stage of denial. Some may, but more often than not, the partner already has known something has been wrong and begins to put together the pieces of times, events and people.

Partners will spend most of their time in the anger stage. This anger can last anywhere from six weeks to six months. They will be mad at what they have lost because of the pretty picture that they thought they had or the security they had, or the feelings they've had of knowing who you were and trusting you. I would encourage you to encourage them to get therapy if they need it and read the book Partners: Healing From His Addiction. It is important for you to understand that their grief is real and this anger is not necessarily toward you as a person, but is toward your addiction. Depersonalizing for you is going to be important so that you don't attack back or do other things that are going to agitate their grief process.

Encourage your partner to go to COSA or SAnon groups to gain support and allow that group setting of relating to their plight to help alleviate some of her anger and grief. They will probably need to have their own therapy sessions about the addiction and behavior so that they can be free to grieve appropriately. With some time and your hard work, she can go through the grief and healing she needs to experience. On the other side, you both have a hope of experiencing the final freedom together.

DANGEROUS DEPRIVATION

Deprivation is a state that a sex addict keeps himself in which deprives him from having legitimate needs met. Sex addicts often will have several areas of deprivation in his life. This is an essential element to identify for a healthy recovery. For some it is their pain agent. It is one of the ways they keep themselves in a state of need. Because their needs are not being met, they believe that they deserve to act out. This is one of the ways the sex addict stays in pain so that he can rationalize his acting out behavior. This is a subtle area that you want to address early in recovery; otherwise you will be in pain, which is the beginning of the sexual addiction cycle. We will look at deprivation several different ways, and learn how it can be prevented so that recovery can be much more successful.

Social Deprivation

Social deprivation is isolating yourself from others. An extreme case would be someone who has no friends and plods through life with their addiction. This happens usually in a later stage of the addiction. Most addicts who do this have low social skills, because their social and emotional needs are being met only by their sexual addiction. Social deprivation will keep you from getting your needs met by people and having friends. It robs you of good feelings about yourself and keeps you in a state of constant pain.

Social isolation can be a way of life for some. I have clients who never developed socially because of their addiction. It is necessary for them to work hard in this area of their recovery so that they will not be socially deprived and stay in the cycle of using sexual behaviors to compensate for this loss.

Spiritual Deprivation

Many sex addicts have difficulty spiritually because it is necessary to be intimate and to have a spiritual relationship with God. God is not afraid to interact with us. But often we may feel like we should be afraid to interact with Him. The guilt and shame of where the addict has been or what they have done, makes it difficult for some addicts to relate to God in an intimate way.

Religion is easy for the sex addict to maintain because it is their front or picture so that no one questions their life-style. Spiritual deprivation can leave the addict feeling alone and disconnected from others. This deprivation often makes him question why he is here and what he is supposed to do. This deprivation is important to work on in recovery because otherwise the addict can say that God doesn't want me, God can't use me. These are rationalizations. If you believe these rationalizations, you can disconnect because there are no consequences for your behavior. You won't have to face a loving God who grieves at your underdevelopment, pain and abuses. You won't be able to sense His love and compassion because of your spiritual deprivation.

This is important to look at as you go through your recovery, especially as you go through your second and third steps. As one person said, "God hasn't moved, we did." Spiritual deprivation can be used as a way to rationalize addictive behavior.

Sexual Deprivation (Sexual/Intimacy Anorexia)

This sounds like a contrary thought, that a sex addict could keep himself sexually deprived. Some sex addicts move in behavior swings. They may not act out for several months and then go on binges and then deprivation again. Another form of sexual deprivation goes deeper. In understanding that sex is spirit, soul and body in a committed relationship, many never get what I call the gold medal in sex. Some may get the bronze or silver medal. What is happening is that the sex addict doesn't get his sexual needs met because he isn't being intimate with his partner. He still has the core belief that "If you knew me, you wouldn't love me." This is especially true if he has affairs during his marriage. Many sex addicts sexually deprive themselves with their spouses (sexual anorexia) and yet are regularly acting out sexually with themselves. They would say they wanted sex frequently, but only would have it once every two to three months. They were keeping themselves in a state of deprivation of sex with a committed person. This would lead them to rationalize that they are not getting sex with their partner. But they are not looking at themselves and their responsibility to be emotionally supportive, kind or loving. They may not even look at the fact that they don't pursue their spouse sexually at home, however the rationalizations continue. I'm in pain; therefore I can rationalize, support or justify my acting out behavior regardless of what it is.

This sexual system needs to be addressed in recovery along with the sex addict's role in the system they have co-created with his partner. If you are disconnected during sex, your partner is not going to want this kind of non-relational sex.

Fun

I have spent countless times asking sex addicts what they do for fun and see their amazed faces again and again as if to say, "What do you mean?" The concept of fun is foreign to many sex addicts. This is primarily due to the fact that most of their entertainment needs are usually in their sexual addiction, whether it be fantasy or acting out with others. This is their "fun" outlet. You won't see other outlets for fun with the sex addict. The addiction has become the primary way of getting their "fun" need met.

Having fun is a legitimate need. Everyone needs to have fun on a regular basis. Without it, the joy of life, creativity, and spontaneity can grow dim, which can set you up for deprivation. The rationalization is, "I'm not having any fun." They may be working too much, blame the kids, or their spouse, or anyone but themselves as to why they are not having fun. This deprivation is sometimes planned. Maintaining this for sometimes weeks at a time can move someone into a binge of acting out behaviors. Someone who doesn't have much fun in their life needs to evaluate why they are keeping themselves in deprivation. We weren't made to be boring. As we look at our early recovery, we need to look at the aspect of fun as far as designing it and having it. Give yourself permission to experience it. If this is an area of weakness I strongly recommend reading my book called The Power of Pleasure. This book helps you identify what brings you pleasure and how to get that pleasure in your life.

Love Deprivation

Being deprived of love is a painful experience. Because of the core belief that "If you knew me you wouldn't love me," most addicts don't believe they are lovable. Sometimes they loathe themselves. Their memories are recorded. When someone doesn't feel lovable and has convinced themselves of this, when real love is around, they discount it. I remember after being married for a few years, one night after a discussion with my wife, I asked her if she loved me. When she said she did, it was the first time I really realized that she loved me. She married me, we had a good marriage, but somehow I couldn't let it in. This deprivation can keep us in trouble. If we don't believe that we are being loved by others, such as our family, friends, we keep ourselves empty--not because others aren't trying to put gallons and gallons of love in there. It is because we've got the door closed. No matter how much love is around us, as long as our door is closed, we can't experience it. Without experiencing it, we don't believe that it is true. Once we come to that conclusion, we are in a lot of pain because we are living without love. Living without love is lonely, boring and can be painful. These feelings and experiences lead us to a point of deprivation where we say, "Nobody cares, and I don't care." So the sex addict abandons themselves to their addiction. They do whatever the addiction pleases, because there they can believe they are loved. In the altered state or fantasy world, they have conditioned themselves to believe that they are loved unconditionally. This has nothing to do with reality.

Intimacy Deprivation

Intimacy is similar to love but has more to do with emotions and the ability to share your heart. Our counseling center is named Heart to Heart because I believe that these are heart to heart issues. A sex addict does not generally have the ability to identify and communicate feelings. That is why they are called frozen feelings until the addict gets into recovery for 30 to 60 days and begins to thaw out. It could take several months to master those feelings and embark on a journey of intimacy. In the beginning, the addict does not feel connectedness, but instead has something I call "the glass wall" around them, leaving them inside and everyone else outside. People can't get to them, so they are safe, but they can't get to themselves either so they feel desperate. They don't know how to meet the needs of others and they feel inadequate. The lack of intimacy is deprivation because all human beings need to touch and be touched. It is important to get this need met through the recovery group and healing. The "Feeling Exercise" in 101 Practical Exercises for Sexual Addiction Recovery alone can help open the door to intimacy. Also, you might want to read any of our marriage books, Intimacy: A 100 Day Guide to Lasting Relationships, The Ten Minute Marriage Principle, and The 7 Love Agreements.

Physical Deprivation

Sex addicts vary on this particular aspect of deprivation and physical deprivation may not apply to all addicts. Regular exercise is a way to get our stress reduced, which is important because stress is a precursor to acting out for many sex addicts. Many have heard the expression H.A.L.T., which stands for Hungry, Angry,

Lonely, Tired. These are some of the stronger feelings that stress the sex addict out and make him more vulnerable to acting out. Physical exercise is one of the things he can do so that he is in good health and has a better attitude about recovery. Exercise will also help endorphins and enkephalins move in the brain so that he has a steady influx of them without it being from sexual acting out behaviors. It can be a healthy balancing opportunity. If the sex addict doesn't exercise, he can put himself in a state of physical deprivation by continuing to work hard, stay up late, and make the body toxic.

As we have discussed before, pain needs medicine. Physical pain especially needs physical medicine. So, if you are not exercising, you are setting yourself up for the physical pain medicine, sexual addiction. You will need to look at this aspect in your recovery and how you can meet this need and move along. We can see that many have unmet needs. It will take time to develop this in your recovery.

Financial Deprivation

Finances seem to be an issue for most sex addicts. With the issue of being in debt and the burden of that debt, they compulsively spend more money. The addict tries to pay off debt to compensate for this and has to use credit cards to pay for groceries. These are cycles in which many sex addicts find themselves. They need to have self restraint by looking at the budget and paying off debt. Put aside entertainment funds so you and your partner can have fun on a regular basis. Set aside funds for Christmas gift buying and going on a vacation. Get a plan that is manageable and be accountable to someone for it.

The Importance of Deprivation

The reason deprivation is so important is because for many sex addicts, it is unawareness that blinds them. This blindness sets them up for so much pain. When they are in that overwhelming sense of pain without knowing what they are feeling, they get confused. In that confusion, their addiction becomes the way out. The addict feels entitled to act out, and he does. Then he is filled with guilt and shame from the consequences of the behavior which will set him up again in the addiction cycle.

Understanding that deprivation is a prelude to pain which begins the addiction cycle is important. If we can look at deprivation in our life and manage it, we will be less likely to be blind-sided by pain. The addict needs to look further into the fact that he is the only one able to meet that need. I remember specifically thinking that I didn't have many male friends in my life. I had acquaintances but not deep friendships. This, I felt, was a legitimate need so I made myself responsible for the need and came up with a plan. I thought of several men who had things in common with me and asked them to do something as a group to see if we got along. Three very significant relationships developed. I feel a sense that my need for friendship is being met in those relationships. I had to look at this, and I had to be responsible for my need. I didn't blame my wife or anyone else. When I made a plan and actively pursued the plan, the results followed.

The deception of deprivation is that if you stay in pain in major areas of your life, you will tend to believe the deception of the rationalizations such as you deserve it, nobody cares, you're not loved anyway. These are all lies but you can't see that early in recovery because you have believed the lies for so many years. Now I can say that I know I am loved, and I don't have to hurt myself, or my family, or be a victim. I now know I can have as much fun as I want along with intimacy, and you can too.

Look at this deprivation early in your recovery because the blind-siding effect of your deprivation can hurt you. Identify it and take responsibility for it and make a plan, get accountable to the plan, and you will find yourself in a better place.

Steps to Change Deprivation

1. Identify and check off the areas of deprivation that apply in your life.

☐ Socially
☐ Spiritually
☐ Sexually
☐ Fun
☐ Love
☐ Intimacy
☐ Physically
☐ Financially

2. Identify the rationale to acting out. List as many of the rationalizations in these areas of deprivation that you currently believe you have, so that you are aware of them when they come up in the future.

3. Identify patterns and length of time or geography for the acting out. Some addicts have 2 to 3 day, week or month patterns. Some act out only when they go out of town or their partner goes out of town. Make yourself accountable to your recovery group sponsor or therapist.

4. Look at the areas of deprivation and write down realistic goals and begin to meet those needs. For example: Fun-If you are a golfer, write down that you will play once or twice a month to start. Start off slowly and realistically. Let your sponsor or therapist know your goals so that they can help keep you accountable for them.

THE TWELVE-STEPS

Now we enter into the recovery program known as the Twelve-Steps. The original Twelve Steps were written many years ago for Alcoholics Anonymous. These alcoholics, after some period of sobriety, decided to write down the principles and the steps they took to maintain their sobriety and to live a healthier life. These principles and steps have been used throughout the world to help millions of people with various addictions such as narcotic abuse, overeating, emotional problems, co-dependency, and sexual ad diction.

The Twelve-Steps of Alcoholics Anonymous Adapted for Sexual Addicts

1. We admitted we were powerless over our sexual addiction, and that our lives had become unmanageable.
2. Came to believe that a power greater than ourselves could re-store us to sanity.
3. Made a decision to turn our will and our lives over to the care of God, as we understood God.
4. Made a searching and fearless moral inventory of ourselves.
5. Admitted to God, to ourselves, and to another human being the exact nature of our wrongs.
6. Were entirely ready to have God remove all these defects of character.
7. Humbly asked God to remove our shortcomings.

8. Made a list of all persons we had harmed and became willing to make amends to them all.

9. Made direct amends to such people wherever possible, except when to do so would injure them or others.

10. Continued to take personal inventory, and when we were wrong, promptly admitted it.

11.Sought through prayer and meditation to improve our conscious contact with God as we understood God, praying only for knowledge of God's will for us and the power to carry that out.

12.Having had a spiritual awakening as the result of these steps, we tried to carry this message to others, and to practice these principles in all our day to day living.

Note: The Twelve-Steps are reprinted and adapted with permission of Alcoholics Anonymous World Services, Inc. Permission to reprint and adapt the Twelve-Steps does not mean that AA has reviewed or approved the content of this publication, nor that AA agrees with the views expressed herein. AA is a program of recovery from alcoholism. Use of the Twelve- Steps in connection with programs and activities which are patterned after AA, but which addresses other problems, does not imply otherwise.

An Interpretation of the Twelve-Steps for Sexual Addicts

What we will attempt to do in the following pages is to explain the principles and concepts of the Twelve-Steps as they are used for recovery from sexual addiction, so that you can implement them in your personal recovery. Our comments here should not be construed as representing any particular Twelve-Step fellowship. They are my own interpretation of the steps from my own experience, as well as from more than twenty years of clinical experience helping sex addicts recover by utilizing the Twelve-Step process.

STEP **1**   We admitted we were powerless over our sexual addiction and that our lives had become unmanageable.

We. I am so glad that the first word in the first step is "we." I would hate to think I was the only person who ever went through this. Sexual addiction is an international as well as a national problem. "We" means that we have similar experiences and we are alike. We grew up in the same family thousands of miles apart. We had the same kind of partners, sexual experiences, abuses and neglects. We is a comforting word in this step. You can see that you are not alone and don't have to be alone. You can get better if you decide to get together. We is an encouraging word and is also essential. Without each other, we often fail to recover.

Admitted. This is a difficult word. Many of us have had situations in our childhood that we have had to admit. Maybe we stole something or something happened to us and we had to admit what we did. Do you remember those feelings of dread before we admitted something? Then we went ahead and admitted it. We told what we did or what happened to us. After we admitted it, we felt less heavy or burdened and as if we could now move on. Admitting for the sexual addict is one of the hardest things we will do in our recovery. Admitting is a very important aspect of recovery and only those who admit to sexual addiction can move forward in recovery and life.

We Were Powerless. Again, I'm glad that there is a "we" in there and that I'm not the only one who is powerless. When we talk about power, we talk about control. Authority, strength or force gives us the ability to be over someone else. But that is not what this word is. This word is powerless and as we know, the suffix "less" means without--such as jobless. This is a tough reality for every addict. We are without any strength, power, control or force to influence our addiction. This is why we need each other and a recovery program. Sometimes that is why we need therapy. We are powerless. We have tried not to sexually act out without success.

The Sex Addict. The sexual addict is dependent on sex to deal with past pain and current stress. If sex is okay, then everything is okay, and as you know, there never is enough sex and we never really are okay. There seems to always be chaos and confusion.

The sex addict is someone whose soul is in pain. If it wasn't, they wouldn't have this addiction. Many sexual addicts, as mentioned earlier, have been sexually or emotionally abused. Many have other additional addictions such as alcohol, drugs or nicotine. A sexual addict is a complicated human being -- a human being in pain.

And That Our Lives. Our lives can be many things. It can be our physical, emotional, intellectual or spiritual life. If you look at all the parts of our lives, they wouldn't equal the totality of our lives. Our lives are the very core of us. It is the inner part of us that identifies us as being separate from another person. This is what has been affected as we look at our sexual addiction. This is the part that feels disconnected, alone, confused and isolated when needs are not being met. It is this part of us that we are going to admit something very important about.

Had Become. These two words indicate to me that this has taken a while. It means that it took time, energy, process and choices. It didn't just happen. It took a while and then eventually, it was made. Your life didn't become overwhelming or devastated instantly, but over a period of time.

Unmanageable. When we think about manageable, we think about things being in order or serene. We can tell when we walk into a store whether the store is manageable or unmanageable. This word means unorganized and chaotic. If someone came from the outside and saw this, they would say "What a mess!" Sometimes this is the way we feel, and our feelings can be valid. Our lives in many of the areas we have talked about have become unmanageable, unconnected, uncontrollable, and unpredictable. No matter how hard we have tried to make them look good or perfect, they don't and they are not. Our lives have become empty and hollow in many respects. Now, through Step One, if we can admit this unmanageability, we have a strong hope of recovery.

I encourage everyone to take Step One seriously because it is the foundation of the Twelve Step program. It will cause you to have a good house of recovery to live in for the future.

For further step work on Step One and all of the Twelve-Steps for Sexual Addicts, I encourage you to use Steps to Freedom: A Twelve Step Guide For Sexual Addiction Recovery. This guide is specifically for sex addicts.

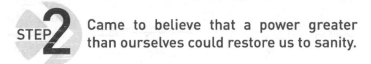 **STEP 2** Came to believe that a power greater than ourselves could restore us to sanity.

Came to Believe. Again, notice the step is written in the past tense. The original steps were written to share the process that the original members of AA went through in recovery. There was a process through which they came to believe.

It is really a simple process. You come to believe many things during your lifetime. For example, you came to believe that there was a Santa Claus. Later you came to believe that there wasn't a Santa Claus. As you grew older, you may have come to believe that a certain person liked you, and later realized they didn't like you. We come to believe certain religious and political positions. There is some consistency to this process throughout our lives. In this process, there is a definite point at which you understand or come to believe.

In Twelve Step groups, the process of coming to believe is something that often happens as a result of exposure to other recovering people. You may not necessarily know the date or the hour when you did come to believe, but you know that you feel differently, and you begin to have hope. This is so important in recovery, because knowing that you have come to believe, or knowing you do believe can save your life. Sex addicts can get down, feel hopeless or worth- less, experience severe shame and guilt from past traumas or present circumstances, and resort to sad behaviors of destruction, isolation, sexual acting out and suicidal ideation. If you have come to believe, you have hope that God cares for you, loves you and accepts you.

A Power. "A" is a common word. You use it every day. A cat, a dog, a book--and in every context in which it is used, it denotes one. If you were going to use a word to describe more than one, you would say "these," or another word that indicates plurality. This step is not written in the plural. It says "a" power greater than ourselves. This is significant. Being an "a" here, you realize that there is one entity, one strength, one energy, one spirit, one power. It is significant that as you come to believe, you are believing in one.

Greater Than Ourselves. This is one of the first areas which requires trust from the sex addict. We now know that there is one that is greater than ourselves. This is the best news we have in recovery, that we don't have to figure this out alone. As you begin to trust this power, you begin to recover from the sick patterns, poor choices, and undesirable relationships that have been so much a part of your past.

In the original context of AA, this power greater than ourselves indicated that the power was greater than that first group of recovering alcoholics. This one single power was greater than a whole group. That's a lot of power. People in recovery frequently first recognize this power in the group, but in reality it is greater than the group. Even if you had a power greater than yourself, you may have had difficulty accessing the resources of that power and applying them to your life. In the program, you come to believe that this power has more ability to solve life's problems than you do individually. What a relief!

Could. "Could" is one of the most helpful, loving expressions in the Twelve-Steps. Could this power have the ability, the resources, the energy, the intention of helping you along in the recovery process? It is possible now to begin to be restored. It is possible now to begin to be healthy, to have loving relationships with loving people, to be loved and nurtured in a healthy way. It can be done, and this power can do it. It is the experience of many in sexual addiction recovery that, if given the freedom and the opportunity--in other words if you quit trying to do it all on your own--this power will do for you what you have been unable or unwilling to do for yourself. All you have to do is ask.

Restore Us to Sanity. "Restore" means bringing something back. Frequently when you think of restoration, you think of restoring an automobile or an old house, and making it look like new. The same is true of sexual addiction recovery.

Sex addicts have for so long been robbed of spirituality, intimacy, trust, and even their own reality. In a world that should have been safe, we violated ourselves again and again.

Insanity is natural when you live with a disease as crazy as sexual addiction. You may have difficulty applying the idea of insanity to yourself, but often having two life-styles at the same time and living with the secret can make most sex addicts feel insane. You try again and again to do something that should work, but doesn't. You try and try to fix the problems that sexual addiction creates in your life without success.

The behaviors themselves are insane, but the fact that you use them again and again, never stopping to realize that they're not working, qualifies you to be restored to sanity. It is possible for sex addicts to be restored to sanity. Those already in recovery have experienced it. They are living proof that it is possible to make better choices, and we hope, as you read this, you know that it is possible for you. You may still feel crazy, but if you have gotten this far in your recovery, you have a good chance at finding sanity.

 STEP 3 Made a decision to turn our wills and our lives over to the care of God, as we understood God.

Made. "Made" is kind of like "became." It indicates a process which involves time and choices, but there is definitely a time when it is done. For example, when kids in school make an ashtray, or a meal in home economics, or a dress, there is a time when it is in the process of being made, and then it is completed. It is made.

"Made" is something that has been coming along, but is finally resolved to the point that you can say it is done.

A. Here again we come to that little word, "a." It is one. What we are discussing in Step Three is a onetime event. Many people want to spread this step out, but as you move along in this process of working the steps, you will see why we only make this decision one time.

Decision. When you make a decision, you list the good and the bad, the pros and cons of a situation. In this step, you can make a list of what you have done with your life in the past, and how you could deal with your life differently in the future. Such a list makes it easier to make the decision you are asked to make in Step Three. It is a decision.

Compare it to a traditional courtship and marriage. It is like you had an engagement period in Step Two, during you make a commitment to share your life with God. You just have a single ceremony, but it sets the stage for further development through the relationship. Step Three asks you to be willing to share your life with God. The decision is a onetime event, but it provides a means for further growth.

To Turn. Turning can be expressed in many ways. Someone said once that turning means "to flip over," kind of like a hot cake. The hot cake gets done on one side, and then you have to turn it over.

It is a pretty simple definition of turn, but it is also pretty profound. If you flip over, you make a total turn or change from the way you have been up to this point.

"Turn" is used on highways all over the world to indicate direction: signs may indicate a left or right turn, or U-turn. When you make a U-turn, you turn around and go in the opposite direction. What you do in Step Three is definitely a U-turn! You turn away from your limited understanding of how life should be. You leave behind perceptions, experiences, and ideas about things you thought you understood. You turn from them and gain a whole new perspective. This is an essential part of recovery. You are turning into something, or turning somewhere else, and it is amazing how far that turn can take you, as you continue in your recovery efforts.

Our Will. Again, this is plural, as the group stays and works together. In this group of safe people, who have turned their wills and lives over to God, you will begin to see this decision as a possibility for yourself. But what is your will? The simplest definition of "will" is probably the ability to make the choices you do for your life. In the group, you will begin to turn over the choices that you make to God. This can be an easy thing for some, but for others it can be a very hard thing to do. It means you must turn your choices over to God, try to understand God's perspective, and follow that perspective in your life. That is why Step Three is so powerful.

As I have mentioned before, in many recovery groups there is a phrase called "stinking thinking." Stinking thinking is the way an addict, alcoholic or a non-recovering person thinks. This thinking doesn't work. The choices non-recovering people make don't bring about positive results. There seems to be a certain self-destructiveness to their choices and behavior. Step Three cuts to the core of stinking thinking. It is the beginning of a new life-style.

Giving up their wills is a safety valve for sex addicts. In making decisions about relationships, they are now able to turn to God. As they do, God will demonstrate new directions they can take, and new choices they can make. They will begin getting answers, and will be able to make different choices about their sexual behavior. This is a freedom that is only gained by letting go of their own will, or choices.

Our Lives. Our lives are the result of all our choices. For each individual, life is the totality of all parts. When you turn it all over--spiritually, emotionally, physically, socially, financially and sexually--you give yourself to God. You begin to trust God. You begin to believe that God will take care of you.

You may say this is frightening: "How can I trust God?!" But simply look at what you have trusted in the past. You have trusted your own ability to think, your own ability to make choices. You have taken the advice of a few chosen people who have not necessarily acted in your best interests.

Turning your will and life over is necessary. It is through this trust experience with God that you begin to believe that God loves you. You begin once again to trust yourself. Eventually, you can even regain your trust in people. Step Three is an essential part of working the steps. It is not a luxury. It is necessary for a healthy, happy life. Working the steps is not always easy, and often you do not understand why you must work them. Often the steps are understood only after they have been completed. Then you realize the beauty of this spiritual process, and open yourself to further growth and joy as you walk this road with others who are making the same steps toward recovery.

The Care of God. What do you think of when you hear the word "care?" It is often expressed in terms of someone who loves you, someone who demonstrates some kindness toward you, someone who is willing to get involved in your life, willing to get in there and be patient with you to work with you and not condemn you in the process; someone who can be nurturing. All these pictures of a loving parent or a loving friend can represent care. Care is felt in the release of energy from one person to another, usually through kind behaviors, like providing a listening ear or some other sign of concern.

How does this relate to God? What is the care of God? It is simply God's willingness to be involved in a nurturing, supportive, accepting way in your life. God is concerned for sex addicts. God's concern for others in this world demonstrates that care. You can sometimes see it more clearly in the lives of others than you can in your own life. For some sex addicts, the group is a manifestation of the care of God in their lives. It is possible for you, by looking at others in your support group to connect with this issue in such a way that it radically changes your life. Something as simple as their support can be seen as the extension of God's care and concern.

Now, we'll talk about God. The original writers of the Twelve-Steps changed only one word from the initial version. In Step Two they changed the word "God." to "a Power greater than ourselves." That is the only change they made, and it was made for this reason: Those first alcoholics said that God was too scary for the recovering person in Step Two. Maybe the recovering person had too many hurts, too many problems with God, so the word was changed to "a Power greater than ourselves" to give the newcomer an engagement period, and allow them to experience God through the group's care, nurturing and love. In this way they could come to believe in a caring God who could, and would, help them.

But who is God? Let me share my thoughts with you on this subject. Simply put, God is Love. God is also in authority or in control, especially for those who turn their lives and will over to Him, and switch the authority from themselves to God.

According to what you have learned so far in the steps, God has the ability to restore you. God is more powerful than you are alone, or in a group. God is one who gets actively involved in your life, who has more power and more success than you in dealing with sexual addiction. This God can and will help you as you work the Twelve-Steps.

For many, this understanding of God will develop into a faith that is common in the American culture, and will enable the recovering sex addict to enjoy the benefits of finding a community that shares the same faith. Some will not. It is a universal blessing of this program, however, that they will, if they are willing to come to a greater relationship with God as they understand God.

The people who have turned their wills and lives over to the care of a God they understand--who have turned their choices over to God--often have more understanding of how God works and how God thinks. The group is a good resource, especially for those early in recovery who want an understanding of God. It is very important to realize, as it pertains to understanding God, that no single person is going to understand the totality of God, but the members of your support group can be helpful in this journey.

As We Understood God. One way to interpret this is to compare your understanding of God with the way you function in relationships with people, because we are talking about a relationship. When you first meet someone, your knowledge of them is limited. Only through time, communication, and commitment to any relationship do you really come to understand another person. The same is true in your relationship with God. Coming to understand God is a process which is available to any and all in recovery who are willing to turn their wills and lives over, so that they can experience a new life, a new freedom, and find happiness. The beauty of finding God in the Twelve-Steps is that as you grow, your understanding of God grows too.

 STEP 4 Made a searching and fearless moral inventory of ourselves.

Made A Searching. Searching holds the possibility of fun, but for sex addicts, searching can be extremely painful. When you search, you intend to find something. For example, when you lose your keys, you go searching, with the intent of finding the keys. As you begin your search inventory, you are searching, you are scrutinizing, you are seeking with intent to find something that is quite significant.

In this context, "searching" indicates that you will have to expend some energy. This is the beginning of what is often referred to in the program as the "action steps." You now begin to take action in your own behalf. Note that this step is also in the past tense. As you begin your inventory, you can know that others have passed this way before, and have survived and gotten better. You are not alone.

Fearless. "Fearless" simply means without fear. This is the attitude with which you approach your moral inventory. Being fearless allows you to view your inventory objectively, as you uncover the pain. You will be looking at what was done to you, and what you have done to yourself and others.

Many of the experiences you will be looking at are extremely painful. For some, the painful experience was childhood sexual abuse, for others it was forced oral sex or rape. For some, it will be something they would much rather not ever remember, something they may think they only imagined. Fearlessness will lead you to look at your own part in the sick relationships you have been in as an adult, and at the patterns that have been repeated over and over in your life. You need to look at these things with an attitude of courage and bravery You can, because in Step Three you turned your will and life over to the care of a loving God.

Moral. "Moral" can be defined as right and wrong, categories of black and white, or good and bad. Something that is immoral could be defined as something that violates your conscience. As you look at your life in Step Four, you will be looking for things that you've done that have violated your conscience. For example, as children, many of us had were not supposed to get a cookie. There might not be anything wrong with having a cookie, but we were told not to, so it became wrong. Yet we waited until our parents could not see, and took a cookie anyway. It probably tasted good, but we may have felt badly afterward. We felt badly because we knew we did something wrong.

In Step Four, you will also be looking at how you were violated by others. Have you ever said to yourself, "If they really knew me, they wouldn't like me. If they knew I was sexually abused or raped, they wouldn't be my friend." The shame and guilt you carry from the actions of other people toward you can be overwhelming. Step Four is designed to release you from that shame and guilt as you look at how your moral code has been violated by others.

It is wrong to believe that you are unworthy because of your past. In recovery, you come to know yourself and let others know you. Step Four is about coming to know yourself, being honest with yourself about what happened, taking into account how it affected your life, and where it leaves you today. In short, Step Four is an inventory. You will list everything that happened, even if it involved others and you were simply an innocent bystander--as in the case of the divorce of parents, or the death of a grandparent or other significant family member.   Such an event may not have had anything to do with your morals, but it did affect you emotionally.

Inventory. What are you to inventory in Step Four? You inventory your experiences because, as a human being, that is what you have on hand. You inventory your memory, for that is what you have been given to record your experiences. Many see this inventory as a life story. It is a process where you begin to see the truth of what you've done, and what has been done to you. Some things will be negative, others will be positive. When a storekeeper takes inventory, he lists not only the things he wants to get rid of, but the things he wants to keep. And he doesn't just make a mental note of it he writes it down.

Step Four is a written assignment. You will need to have pen or pencil, paper, and a quiet place where you can be uninterrupted. Some just begin writing. Some organize their inventory by ages, such as zero-to six years, seven to twelve years, and so on. Still others have done it by first listing all the traumatic events they can remember--things that were done to them or by them that violated their value system--and then writing how they felt at the time, and how they feel now about those events. There is no right or wrong way to write an inventory. The important thing is just to do it. You will be face to face for perhaps the first time with the total reality of your life.

It can be pretty overwhelming, so don't be afraid to let your sponsor or therapist know how you are feeling while writing your inventory. As you transfer your story to paper, you are also transferring the pain, guilt and shame onto paper. Writing an inventory can be a very positive transforming experience, and it is vital to your recovery.

Of Ourselves. Once again, you can see this is plural. You can know that others have done this before. You can survive the pain of writing your inventory down. It is joyous to see others freed from their shame. As you see other members of your support groups complete their inventories, you will begin to believe that this release from shame can happen for you too. You are reminded that only you can do this for your- self. Only you know your pain, the strength of your fears, your deepest secrets. Only you are qualified to write this inventory. Now is the time to decide for yourself who you are, and who you want to be. There is great freedom in taking your focus off what is wrong with others, and doing a searching and fearless moral inventory of yourself. You may not understand the value of this step until you have completed it, but it is well worth the pain and tears.

 STEP **5**   Admitted to God, to ourselves, and to another human being the exact nature of our wrongs.

Admitted. Here you are again, looking at that word, "admitted." You already know that it means to "fess up," or acknowledge what is already true. You may have already experienced the pain and joy of doing this, probably as a child or adolescent. Perhaps you put yourself in a situation you knew your parents would not approve, or did something wrong, and knew you were going to have to tell them, because you knew they were going to find out anyway. Do you remember your feelings of guilt and shame, like you had let yourself and them down? Then you somehow got the courage to tell them what you had done. You admitted the truth--no matter the consequences. It felt better, finally, to let the secret out.

The same is true in Step Five. You admit all that you have written in your Fourth Step. You let out all those secrets and finally feel that clean joy which comes from truly being totally known.

To God. God might be the easiest person to tell, or the hardest, depending on your relationship with Him. If you feel God has let you down before, admitting what has been wrong in your life can be particularly difficult. Fortunately, God is forgiving of all that you have done, and is willing to restore any lost part of yourself. As one wise person in recovery stated, "It's okay to tell God. God already knows it all anyway, and is just waiting for us to be honest about it too."

To Ourselves. Admitting your past secrets to yourself often takes place as you write your Fourth Step, if you are truly fearless and thorough when writing it. Admitting your powerlessness, your need to be restored to sanity, your profound amazement at your poor choices, and your sincere sense of having failed yourself is probably the most humbling experience you will have with regard to your sense of who you are.

It is at this point, though, that the recovery of your true self is able to take an upward turn, without the overwhelming sense of shame or guilt that has been so closely bound to you in the past. You are now able to begin a more shame-free life, which empowers you to experience the next and most essential part of this step: being able to reveal yourself to another human being.

And to Another Human Being. "What? I have to tell all this stuff to somebody else, face to face?" Yes, telling your story to another human being is the most crucial part of your recovery. In writing your Fourth Step, you have taken your total history of shame, hurt, abandonment, abuse and poor choices, acting out, and poured it consciously into one place. Your Fourth Step may even have brought to your conscious awareness some things you have been suppressing for years, and now all of these memories are in one place. If all this pain is kept inside you, and is not shared with another human being, you may talk yourself into believing once again that you are unlovable or unacceptable with such a painful, messy past. You could use this negative information and history for condemnation instead of healing. That is why we must tell another person. We must realize that we are loved and accepted even though we have been places and experienced things of which we are not proud.

In this Fifth Step you experience spiritually, emotionally, and often physically, a cleansing or a lightening of your load. As you share who you have been and what you have experienced with another trusted person, you are reassured that nothing you have done makes you unlovable. Now someone knows the whole truth, and still loves you. It is remarkable!

A note of caution is appropriate here: When you choose someone to hear your Fifth Step, it is important to pick the least condemning, most loving and accepting person you know. You might choose a therapist, sponsor or spiritual person you trust. Choose someone who understands that you are digging into your past in order to make your present and future better--someone who will not shame you for your past. This person can be a member of your support group as well. This choice is yours. Make it in your best interest.

The Exact Nature of Our Wrongs. The fact that this part of the step is so specific will help two kinds of people: those who say, "I can't be specific so I'll never really feel loved," and those who believe that they can own everybody else's wrongs and avoid looking at their own choices. The first person needs to be specific in sharing his story, because the shame he experiences about the past is tied to specific episodes. We must talk about those specific episodes to relieve the shame associated with them. The second person needs to acknowledge his own shortcomings and "clean his own side of the street"--not anyone else's--so that he too can be freed from his own shame.

It's a recognized fact that you can't free anyone else from their shame. Each person has to work their own program of recovery in order to have the kind of happy and fulfilling life we are all capable of experiencing. As a note of caution, for those who have violated children, most states demand professionals report if the specific name and place of this event is given to them. In sharing this information be aware of this when doing your Fifth Step.

STEP 6   Were entirely ready to have God remove all these defects of character.

Were Entirely Ready. As you move from Step One through Step Five, you discover a process through which you recognize powerlessness, find a God of your understanding, go inside yourself by writing an inventory, and let someone else know who you really are. The very core of the program is in the first five steps. By working these steps you have learned to "trust God and clean house."

Now that you have cleaned house, you must learn how to maintain your new surroundings. It is one process to clean a dirty house, whether you got it dirty yourself or just inherited all the mess--and it is another thing entirely to make sure that it never gets dirty again. That is what Step Six and the following steps are all about--preventative maintenance.

You start by "being entirely ready." This simply means that you are 100 percent ready to look at the damage that was done by all that trash, and you evaluate what you can throw away. You might be quite attached to some of that stuff.   Even though it doesn't work any longer, you hesitate to give it up. Someday, some of those old behaviors might come in handy, you keep thinking. You forget that each time you try old behavior it causes great pain. "Were entirely ready" indicates that you are finally tired of the pain. You finally realize that changing is not quite as frightening as staying the same.

To Have God. Having God in our lives is so significant for sex addicts. Here in Step Six they are reminded that they, like everyone, are blessed by having a relationship with God. They are beginning to believe that God does want the best for them, and that God wants their lives to express this new way of feeling and believing about themselves. God is willing to work with you, as you continue your efforts at recovery.

Remove All. This sounds like an unrealistic, maybe even painful statement, at least from a human standpoint. "Remove" indicates loss. Sex addicts have certainly experienced loss in their lives. But to lose, or remove, all of their defects? How?

Well, it isn't up to you to decide how, it's only up to you to be ready. Remember that earlier you recognized that you don't have a whole lot of power of your own. In Step Six you will rely on God to have the power to change you--the power you've been unable to access in your addiction.

Defects of Character. As you consider the term, "defects of character," you might be thinking of some of the ways you have behaved and felt that didn't work very well. Go ahead and get a pencil and paper and write down what comes to mind. Reviewing your inventory should give you a good idea of things about your character you might want changed.

For example, perhaps the way you express your anger indicates a defect of character. Maybe the way you control, and try to manipulate, your spouse or children, or the way you pout to get your own way, or isolate or run away from responsibility for yourself, are things you want to change. Honesty is important in listing these defects, because the ones you hold on to will keep you stuck in old patterns, and you will continue to attract unhealthy people into your life, especially in intimate relationships.

It is the experience of recovering sex addicts that as they become more healthy and honest themselves, they gravitate toward more healthy, honest people, and are better able to determine who is unhealthy. Understanding this can certainly motivate you to really look at your defects of character, and be 100 percent willing to have God remove them. This is the real release that prevents the dust and trash from resettling in your house.

 STEP 7   **Humbly asked God to remove our shortcomings.**

Humbly. Many struggle with the word, "humble," having been humiliated time and again by sexual addiction. Humility is not the same as humiliation, although you may feel something like humiliation as you see the devastation in your own life and the lives of those around you caused by your defects of character. Humility, in this case, means recognizing your true humanness. You see in Step Seven the manner with which you should approach God. Humility means knowing that you don't have the power to change yourself, but that God does. You come into God's presence with a humble heart, but with hope as well. And as you ask, you shall receive. As long as you don't have preconceived ideas of just how and when God will remove your defects of character, you will have them removed.

Asked God. Humility requires that we ask, not tell, God anything. By now perhaps you have come to believe that God really does want the best for you; wants you to be free of your defects of character; wants you to feel good about yourself, and to be attracted to healthy people. You are asking, in a sense, to do God's will.

To Remove Our Shortcomings. In Step Six you became ready. Now you push the "Go" button, and ask God to take your defects of character, or shortcomings. It would be nice if it happened all at once, but again you will experience it as a process. In this process, God will be with you throughout your life, removing your shortcomings as you continue to identify them when they surface, as long as you are willing to ask for help.

For some addicts, this step comes easily. For others, it is very hard, especially if you are holding on, still rationalizing, still defending, still gripping your defense mechanisms. In that case, Step Seven can be a painful experience. As someone once said in a meeting, "There was never anything I let go of that didn't have claw marks all over it, including my defects of character."

You can trust that if you ask, God will remove your defects of character, no matter how much you resist. If you decide to hold on to them, you will be fighting a losing battle. It is at this point that you will really need your support group. They will give you valuable feedback about any shortcomings they see you holding on to. If you aren't sure, ask questions.   They will also give you support as you try new behaviors in place of the old ones that kept you so unhappy. Allow them to support you in this growth process.

STEP 8 Made a list of all persons we had harmed, and became willing to make amends to them all.

Made A List. You probably don't have any problem shopping for groceries if you've made a list. You know that the most efficient way to shop is to have a written list, instead of just mental notes, because otherwise you are likely to get home and find you have forgotten some essential items. There is a saying in Alcoholics Anonymous that you should be fearless and thorough from the very start. This is true in Step Eight. Again, take a pencil and paper in hand, and looking at your inventory, make a list of all those you have harmed. This list should include yourself as well as others, and can also include what damage was done, and the person's name.

Of All Persons. Here again is that sometimes scary word: all. "All" means every single one. You are, once again, being challenged to be honest. To the degree that you can be honest in making this list, you will have hope for new relationships with important people in your life.

We Had Harmed. It takes an honest person to look at their life and see the people they have harmed. It is often easier to see how you have been harmed by others. In Steps Four and Five, you looked at how you have been hurt by trusted people in your life; how you have been traumatized; how you have been emotionally abandoned; and how you have suffered. But if all you look at is how you have been harmed, you are only halfway healed.

Just as it can be painful for a recovering alcoholic to see how his drinking damaged those around him, so it can be painful for the recovering sex addict to realize what he has done to hurt others. For many sex addicts, it is much more comfortable to be the victim. As a matter of fact, they have often been the victim of their own behavior, of their own past, and even of recent relationships. But past victimization by others just makes it that much more difficult for these people to realize that they have actually harmed other people. The acting out behavior is just the start of this list. The harm can be very subtle. You need to really search your mind and heart, in order to complete your healing.

And Became Willing. The past tense here reminds you, one more time, that the hard work demanded in the previous steps is survivable. Sex addicts have worked their way through these steps before, and have found peace and happiness on the other side. It also indicates a process. Recovery doesn't just happen overnight. Becoming willing takes time for everyone, especially if they are holding on to a victim status.

To Make Amends. What does it mean to make amends? For sex addicts, or anyone in recovery for that matter, to make amends means to acknowledge the wrong they have done, and be willing to be different. You stop blaming the other person to justify your own behavior. You stop rationalizing, and defending yourself. You stop avoiding responsibility. You are continuing to change in your relationships with yourself and others. You take full responsibility for what you have done, and to whom you have done it, at least on paper at this point.

To Them All. Here is that word "all" again. It seems to appear everywhere throughout the steps. By now your list should include everyone who has in any way been harmed by your actions or lack of actions. You should have found the willingness to be different with each person on that list, including yourself. No stone should be left unturned at this point, or you will still carry old guilt that will keep you stuck in old sick patterns of thinking and relating. With names, phone numbers, and accounts of damages in hand, you are ready to move on.

STEP 9   Made direct amends to such people wherever possible, except when to do so would injure them or others.

Made Direct Amends. In Step Eight, you made your list. Now you go to the grocery store. In Step Nine, you actually go to the people on your list and make direct amends to them for the inappropriate attitudes or behaviors you have had in the past that have affected them. Notice again that this step is written in the past tense. These steps were written in the late 1930s when the first members of Alcoholics Anonymous became sober. Working these steps, especially Step Nine, was something they had to do to maintain their sobriety, so they would not have to carry the pain, shame or guilt of the past or present into their new sober lives.

They had to be honest with themselves. So do you as you go to each person on your list and ask them for their forgiveness. When you acknowledge how your behavior affected your relationships with them, you will find the most incredible freedom. Tremendous emotional weights can be lifted, and often relationships can be restored, as the result of working Step Nine. This is not a 100 percent guarantee, since some relationships will remain fractured. However, at least your side of the street will be clean.

You will begin to feel wholeness and happiness in your life, now that you have made the effort to vent completely, without expectations. This is a significant point: You do not make amends with the expectation that your friends or family will change their behavior. You do not make amends with the expectation that people will respond in any certain way. People may, in fact, respond when you make amends, but it is by no means the motivation for you to do what you must to get rid of what you have been carrying for so long. Inflated expectations can cause you much pain, because others are not always in the same place with their recovery that you are with yours. Many people do not choose a path of recovery at all. Your personal efforts and behavior however, can challenge them into this kind of recovery at some point in the future.

It is not a given that the other person will ask forgiveness in return, even though they may have injured you much more than you have injured them. Your goal is to clean your own slate. You are not responsible for what others leave undone, nor can their shortcomings keep you from recovering and feeling good about yourself.

Except When To Do So Would Injure Them or Others. When you get to this point, you may become confused when you attempt to decide if making amends will injure the person involved, or be detrimental to other, possibly innocent people. Such confusion is best resolved with the assistance of a group, sponsor or therapist. Confusion is not to be used, however, as an excuse to not make any amends because you don't want to experience the pain or shame of admitting your past behavior.

What you must consider when admitting past behavior is whether or not your confession would so significantly damage the other person involved that you should not raise the issue to them. You can ask yourself, "Would this be damaging?" If you have a question, do not assume you have the answer. You could very possibly avoid an amend which could restore a relationship, or hold on to an amend that will set you up for old behavior. Go over your list with a sponsor, support group or therapist if at all possible.

STEP 10 Continued to take personal inventory and when we were wrong, promptly admitted it.

Continued. Here again you must deal with the maintenance of your newly clean house. You are not letting the dust fall. You are not letting the dirt collect, or the garbage overflow in the can. Here you are in a process, as in Steps Four and Five. Today, when you have been inappropriate or have violated anyone's boundaries, including your own, you don't have to wait five or ten years to make amends. You can do it as you go along.

To Take Personal Inventory. Taking a daily personal inventory is a process in which sex addicts are able to look at each person in their life, and see how they are interacting with this person. They look at their attitudes toward others and honestly evaluate them. This is not done to the point where they are unable to enjoy interactions, but it is an honest evaluation of how they respond to peers, family, and in all other relationships. It also is a reminder that you inventory only your own behavior, not anyone else's.

And When We Were Wrong, Promptly Admitted It. You will be wrong. This part of Step Ten says, "When," not, "If," you were wrong. Many sex addicts have been wronged, but there will still be times when you will be wrong yourself. It is so important for the recovering person to stay free, and not enter into a place of guilt and shame, which can push you into some acting out behavior. So, in the maintenance of Step Ten, when you are wrong, you promptly admit it. "Promptly" is significant because it keeps you from holding on to the baggage, thinking for months about whether you were or weren't wrong. Promptly means admit it right now, right here. If you have been acting inappropriately, say, "I'm sorry. Forgive me, I'm acting inappropriately." It is as simple as that. Step Ten gives you a way to stay free from the bondage of guilt and shame. It keeps you humble, which often helps you to remain healthy.

STEP 11 Sought through prayer and meditation to improve our conscious contact with God as we understood God, praying only for knowledge of God's will for us and the power to carry that out.

Sought Through Prayer and Meditation. This step not only tells you what you are doing, but it also tells you how to do it. You are seeking. You are looking to improve your relationship with God. This step tells you to do that through prayer and meditation. Prayer is that verbal, and sometimes internal, communication with God. It is such a positive experience for the sex addict to become more aware of God in his life. This step lets you know that it is your responsibility. Seeking requires action on your part. You may have felt abandoned by God, since you put no real effort into trying to find out where He was. It has been said many times in meetings, "If you can't find God, guess who moved." You move away from God, God never moves away from you. Seeking Him is all that it takes to find Him.

Meditation is a sometimes deeper sense of prayer. Prayer is requesting, asking, interacting. Meditation is listening and hearing God's voice. A lot of humans experience rest and peace through meditation, and are able to still the constant obsessive thinking that prevents them from hearing what God has to say: that they are significant, they are loved, and they deserve to be healthy. Meditate on God's character, on your personal relationship with Him, on some scripture or recovery material you have, and allow them to really sink in to your spirit. Be still, and God will speak to you.

To Improve Our Conscious Contact With God. Most sex addicts, like many people, have an unconscious contact with God. They rely most of the time on their own thinking and resources, and connect with God only after they have thoroughly botched their lives. Step Eleven reminds you to keep God in your conscious mind. You are then able to experience the power and love of God in a whole new way. As a result, you will experience life in a whole new way. You will have a higher sense of purpose and joy. The result of this new awareness of God on a moment to moment basis is a better relationship with God. As with any relationship, efforts at improving the relationship require time, energy, and some sort of communication. With time you will find the method of communication that works best for you. There is no right or wrong way to do it. Just do it.

As We Understood God. It is impossible for any one of us to totally understand God. Indeed, my understanding of God might not work for you, nor yours for me. The beauty of the program is that you can begin to see evidence of God in other people. Remember this is not a job you undertake on your own. You come to a new understanding of God as you interact with the people in your support group, church, or other community of people seeking knowledge of God. As you listen, you will grow in understanding through other people's experiences of God in their lives.

Praying Only For Knowledge of God's Will For Us. By now you are beginning to see the benefits of letting go of self will. In Step Eleven, you are gently reminded that when you pray for God's will in your life, you are asking for the absolute best solution to whatever you are facing. So often we push and push situations to turn out the way we want them to, only to find out that we got second or third or seventh or tenth best. It is a very positive thing to realize that you can trust God to have your best interests at heart. The people, places and things you have given your will over to in the past did not have your best interests at heart. You now trust God enough to say, "Not my will, but thy will be done."

And The Power to Carry That Out. You pray for knowledge of God's will, not just for the sake of having the information, but also for the power to carry it out. Having the information without the willingness or power to carry it out, will not change anything. After prayer for the knowledge, you can now listen in meditation for God to tell you the things you need to do. Sometimes a path will open, sometimes God will bring to mind a defect of character that is getting in your way, and sometimes God will challenge you in the way you are behaving through intuitive thoughts or feelings you may have. Often the power to make the changes God seems to want you to make comes through the people in your support groups. It can even come from seeing someone stuck in old behaviors. You can be motivated to change by seeing the consequences others are experiencing because of their unwillingness to act differently. Once having asked for direction and listened for guidance, you can act with assurance, knowing that if you are on the wrong track, you will come to know it. And you always know that you're not alone.

 STEP 12 Having had a spiritual awakening as the result of these steps, we tried to carry this message to others and to practice these principles in all our day-to-day living.

Having Had A Spiritual Awakening As The Result Of These Steps. It is no wonder that an individual who comes to the steps-

-and in the process of time admits to powerlessness, admits to humanness, admits to the need for a relationship with God, actively pursues that relationship, cleans house, makes amends, and maintains this behavior--has a spiritual awakening. This spiritual awakening is the purpose of working the steps. It is an awakening in which the sex addict discovers he has worth and value that he is loved by God, and can be loved by others, if he will only believe in his lovableness and open up his heart and let that love in.

This awakening to a spiritual connection with God can give the addict the power to change their way of relating to themselves and the world. They can now see themselves as a precious child of a loving God, and treat themselves and others accordingly.

We Tried to Carry This Message to Others. In the beginning of Alcoholics Anonymous, it was not a matter of a drunk alcoholic seeking advice and support from someone who was sober. It was the recovering alcoholic who sought out the active drinker. Bill W., the cofounder of AA, knew that if he couldn't share what he had discovered about his relationship with God and its importance to his sobriety, he wouldn't be able to stay sober. This is true for sex addicts too. As your progress in your recovery, and become less absorbed in your own pain, you begin to recognize when others around you are in pain. You will begin to see opportunities to share your experience, strength, and hope with other sex addicts who are suffering from the same low self esteem, dependency or independency problems, and lack of boundaries that you experienced. And you will share, not to get them well, but to remain mindful of the miracle of recovery in your own life. Without constant reminders, you are likely to forget where your strength and health come from, and become complacent.

One of the truest sayings around recovery groups is, "You can't keep it if you don't give it away." The door to recovery is opened to you because others passed this way before. It is your joy, as well as your responsibility, to keep the door open for those who follow you, and lead them to the door if they can't find it. It is the only way to ensure freedom for all.

And To Practice These Principles In All Our Day-To-Day Living. Here is the most practical part of the Twelve-Steps. Take what you have learned, and keep doing it every day. Practice admitting your powerlessness over the problems in your life. Practice acknowledging God's ability to run your life and keep you from practicing old behaviors. Practice new thinking and behavior skills. Practice prayer and meditation. Like the athlete who must exercise daily to stay in shape, you need to practice daily the new skills you have learned, so you can stay in good emotional and spiritual shape. It took many years of practicing old behaviors for you to end up with such low self esteem and such a lack of boundaries. It will take practice to become the new person you want to be. But it is possible!

Congratulations to all who embark on this journey of the Twelve-Steps. These steps when followed are a tried and true path to the final freedom.

PROFESSIONAL HELPERS

In addition to the vital attendance and involvement in Twelve-Step recovery, many sex addicts benefit greatly from professional therapy.

"What? Am I in need of therapy too?" Does the idea of therapy frighten you? A general discussion of the types of therapy and treatment settings available might help you decide if therapy is for you.

Like the medical or financial fields, the mental health field has various levels of professionally trained people. These professionals have a wide variety of philosophies and training perspectives, and can meet the different needs of sex addicts.

Counselors Certified to Treat Sex Addiction

A certified therapist in sexual addiction recovery trained through the American Association for Sex Addiction Therapists is a Masters level or higher counselor who is licensed by their state. They have undergone a minimum of 45 hours of training by Dr. Weiss. They have been supervised during their training for a minimum of 6 months by Dr. Weiss or a certified supervisor and have completed a competency exam in sexual addiction.

This counselor has invested him or herself to be trained in the field of sex addiction is the best first pick. Make sure they have been trained by AASAT so they will be utilizing the paradigms and assessments that have been tested by time to be successful.

Psychiatrist

Psychiatrists are medical doctors. They attend several years of medical school, and are trained to look at biological reasons for problems with the human being. They are trained in medications that influence the chemistry of the brain. This professional can be a valuable help or support to a sex addict if the addict has been previously diagnosed with a disorder of depression, manic-depression, or other problem that requires the supervision of a medical doctor. He or she can prescribe medication the sex addict might need to feel better, such as antidepressant medication.

If the psychiatrist has had addiction training, or has had exposure to workshops dealing with sexual addiction, he or she may be of some help to you as you work on your issues.

Psychologist

A psychologist is quite different from a psychiatrist, although they are often confused as they both have the designation of doctor. Psychologists are Ph.D., Ed.D., or Psy.D.'s, not medical doctors. They have not attended and graduated from medical school. They are not licensed physicians. Therefore, they cannot prescribe medication. They spend their educational training looking at the cognitive, or thinking, aspects of the human being, such as Intelligence Quotient, reading and math levels, psychological testing, and the like. He or she is often trained to do individual, group and marital therapy.

A psychologist with a doctorate in psychology can be of great help to the sex addict, especially if he or she has had experience working with sex addicts. A psychologist can be of help in therapy to a sexual addict especially if the addict is experiencing any psychological disorder, such as depression, suicidal thoughts, or a compulsive eating, sleeping or alcohol disorder. Often these survival mechanisms respond well to treatment under the care of a trained and licensed psychologist.

Licensed Professional Counselor

The Licensed Professional Counselor, or L.P.C., usually has either masters level training, or Ph.D. level training with expertise in counseling or another field, i.e., sociology or anthropology. They can acquire a counselor's license through taking certain counseling classes. A master's level degree is the minimum required for the L.P.C. in most states. The master's level professional may also have a degree in an area other than counseling, like an M.Ed. (Master's In Education), and take ten or fifteen classes in counseling during or after his or her graduate degree program, to acquire a professional license from the state he or she practices in. This is something to note in your initial interview with a Licensed Professional Counselor. You can ask exactly what their background is, because some licenses may not require a degree in counseling in some states. This can be important for addicts to know when they are seeking help for their own issues or for the issues regarding their family, marriage or children.

The master's level L.P.C., much like a psychologist, can be a great resource for a sex addict as he deals with family and individual problems. An L.P.C. is usually able to identify and deal with depression, obsessive/compulsive disorders, addictive disorders, co-dependency, and other issues. L.P.C.'s, like psychiatrists and psychologists, have ongoing training and, in most states, will have a more reasonable fee structure for those seeking counseling. In finding a Licensed Professional Counselor, ask how many years they have been practicing, and review the "Questions to Ask" section at the end of this chapter, to determine the counselor's experience with sexual addiction treatment.

Social Workers

Social workers will have either a bachelor's or a master's level education. They may have several levels of certification which can differ from state to state. They may be a Certified Social Worker (CSW) or a masters level Social Worker (MSSW), depending on their experience. Their training is mostly from a social perspective. Seeing issues from a social perspective is beneficial, and can be helpful, but unless specific training is given to the Social Worker in the field of addictions, there may be limits as to how helpful they can be. However, if there is a need for social services for the family or for the sex addict--for example, in finding places for residential treatment--a social worker can usually be quite resourceful. In some states the social worker is much like a Licensed Professional Counselor, as they provide individual, group or family therapy. In other states and situations they may do social histories and things of that nature. In finding a social worker, you will need to find out what educational training and experience they have had. You may find that this will be a very beneficial relationship to you, as you seek help for either your own issues or those of your family. Again, refer to the "Questions to Ask" section at the end of this chapter for further information.

Pastoral Counselors

Pastoral counseling is also available in many areas. Pastoral counselors include people who have professional degrees in counseling from an accredited seminary or institution. They may have a doctoral level education (Ph.D.), or they may have master's level education. Pastors of local congregations would be included in this category. Although most pastors minimally have a bachelor's level education, some may have no formal education at all. Such counselors can be significantly helpful to those who have strong church, Christian or religious backgrounds. Pastoral counselors can be very helpful in your recovery, because development of spirituality is a significant part of recovery for the whole person.

The strengths of a pastoral counselor would include his spiritual training, coupled with professional experience and professional training in the fields of addictions, or counseling and psychological training. With such training, a pastoral counselor could be of the utmost benefit.

Some possible weaknesses of the pastoral counselor might be a lack of training or skill in some areas. The pastor who has had no training in counseling may be of brief support to the sex addict, but might not be as beneficial in resolving personal issues or identifying other psychological problems that a sex addict might have. Pastors are usually not trained counselors but can be a great support to the sex addict in the recovery process of sexual addiction as far as accountability.

The pastoral counselor, like all other professionals discussed, should be asked the appropriate questions from the "Questions to Ask" section. This is very important. Often, their understanding of addictions and sexual issues can influence how therapeutic they can be to you.

Christian Counseling

Christian counseling is another form of counseling which is now readily available in most larger cities, as well in some smaller communities. Christian counseling is not exactly the same as pastoral counseling. Many Christian counselors do not hold a position as a pastor, nor will they have professional pastoral counselor education training.

A Christian counselor is often professionally trained in the theory of counseling, psychology and human development. These counselors can be master's or doctoral level trained professionals, but the training that the counselor receives can vary widely. It is wise to check the Christian counselor's training prior to having any therapeutic relationship.

There is a specific benefit in having a Christian counselor for those who embrace the Christian faith. They can be a great source of help, especially if they are able to integrate biblical truths and biblical understanding into the healing process. They can be very supportive and encouraging to the personal development of the sex addict, and can also facilitate growth for the whole family. Again, ask the questions relating to training and expertise in the area of sex addiction. Just because they are Christian does not guarantee they understand or successfully treat sex addiction.

Certified Alcohol and Drug Addiction Counselors or Licensed Chemical Dependency Counselors

CADAC's and LCDC's are available in most areas, although their designations may differ from state to state. These are counselors with a variety of training backgrounds. They may have a Ph.D., a master's or bachelor's degree, or may have had no formal education whatsoever. Again, the training of an individual counselor is very significant. This cannot be stressed more than in the field of alcohol and drug addictions. In some states individuals recovering from alcoholism or drug addiction, who want to enter the helping profession, find that such certification is the easiest way into this field. They do have a valid experience and understanding of the addiction process, as well as understanding of the recovery process. However, caution must be used in that recovering people often have multiple addiction problems. This is something to be noted when interviewing an addictions counselor. In addition, it is important to ask how they have integrated a Twelve Step philosophy into their own lives. Our personal opinion is that unless a counselor has done at least a Fourth and Fifth Step and has begun the process of making amends, his or her perceptions might still be clouded by guilt and shame, and the counselor might not be able to facilitate the growth you need in your life.

Addiction counselors do have some strengths, however. They are often trained in family systems theory. They are familiar with the dynamics of addiction and usually come from a Twelve-Step perspective. Often these counselors can be found working in alcohol and drug addiction treatment centers. Sometimes they office with a psychiatrist, psychologist, or master's level counselor. They are often supervised in their work by a degreed professional. You can ask if the case load is being supervised, and by whom, and what that supervision process is. This is important because some supervisors, due to time constraints, will not review each case thoroughly. Another benefit to an addictions counselor is that he or she would be aware of recovery groups in the area, and the importance of support groups.

Marriage and Family Counselors

Marriage and family counselors can have a variety of degrees in education also. They may have a Ph.D., or a master's degree in marriage and family counseling. For sex addicts, this may or may not be helpful, depending on the situation. If you are in a marriage or a committed relationship, such a counselor can be very beneficial.

Marriage and family counselors come from a family systems approach, taking into consideration the needs of the entire family, and not just the needs of one person. Also, they will be highly attuned to how each family member processes problems, and how the family members interact with each other.

For example, in some addictive systems the addict is the one who is perceived as needing help, the wife is the one who is strong and "helps" the addict, while the children are her supporters, her cheerleaders in helping dad. From a systems approach, a counselor might look at this situation and say, "Dad needs to be sick, so that Mom can be a helper." Mom needs to give up the helper role and establish her own identify and boundaries, so if Dad recovers, the family doesn't need somebody else to be sick, i.e., the children or Mother herself.

The marriage and family counselor will be highly astute in these matters and can be beneficial to the sex addict, as well as to the family as a whole. Refer to the "Questions to Ask" section to determine what training and experience this counselor has in addictions in general, and in sexual addiction specifically, as well as in recovery from sexual addiction.

It is very appropriate to interview the professional you are considering as a therapist. Each addict has a different history, and could have possible conflicts with certain professionals due to their past experiences. Also, the many professionals discussed here represent a sort of continuum of care. At one point in recovery you might find one type of professional more helpful than another. Many practices include several types of therapists, and are able to treat sex addicts from what is known as a multi-disciplinary view. In interviewing a potential therapist, consider the following list of questions.

Questions to Ask

- Do you have experience working with sex addicts?
- How many sex addicts have you seen in the last two months?
- Do you have training to do therapy with people with addictions? (State or Board certification)
- Are you a recovering person working a Twelve-Step program?
- What books have you read on sexual addiction?
- Do you have specific training to deal with (if these issues apply to you) rape victims, survivors of child sexual abuse, incest or other trauma?

Counseling

The current number of professionals who treat sex addiction specifically and with a great deal of success can be limited even in the larger metropolitan area. Heart to Heart Counseling Center has established counseling for the sex addict, the partner of a sex addict, and for couples counseling. For more information or to locate a therapist in your area, contact Heart to Heart Counseling Center at 719-278-3708.

TO MY RELIGIOUS FRIENDS

The Twelve-Steps: Friend or Foe

The Twelve-Steps of Alcoholics Anonymous were founded in the early 1930s. In the history of these groups, you will find that the founders were committed to prayer and spiritual growth. The environment in which these steps were developed was a society and church unaccepting of alcoholics. This group was developed to help support and nurture alcoholics to return them to health and sanity and to have a spiritual awakening, which is the Twelfth Step. The Twelve-Steps were taken from an Oxford Bible Study. They were modified for Alcoholics Anonymous. Many of the Twelve-Step principles are very biblical and supportive of someone desiring to move from sickness or addiction to health and recovery.

The emphasis for the Twelve-Step support groups is not theological. It's practical. It is not a matter of determining your interpretation of the scripture or if your interpretation of God is accurate or theologically sound. The emphasis of the Twelve Step group is whether you are acting out or not. The Twelve-Steps can help lead you into a healing process.

These principles are very spiritual and biblical. I personally have walked through many of the steps before I was ever introduced to the Twelve-Steps through various biblical teachings. The Twelve-Steps can help you. They don't need to be feared, but can be a friend. At this point you need a friend to help you walk through your addiction recovery. The Twelve-Steps can be that friend.

A Support Group

The support groups of Sex Addicts Anonymous, Sex and Love Addicts Anonymous, and Sexaholics Anonymous and various others are there with open arms to help you begin your recovery from sex addiction. Sex addiction affects all walks of life and crosses socioeconomic barriers, and ethnic and religious belief systems. In any culture, you will find sex addicts. The recovering Christian sex addict needs to humble themselves and hear from others who may think differently on some things. They know how not to act out and have weeks, months or years of sobriety, because they have integrated what it takes to learn how to recover. Recovery does have principles that when applied can maintain sobriety. Without these principles, you will probably fail and end up back in your addiction. The people in these groups have the knowledge of these principles. It is similar to going to school and learning something that you want to get a degree in. You learn from people who already know. If you fell in the ocean while you were on a cruise boat, and you were trying to swim while the lifeboat was leaving, and someone was trying to throw you a life jacket, would you say, "No, you're not a Christian. You can't throw me a life jacket."

Most would agree that this is absurd. The belief that someone has to believe exactly the same as you to save your life is not practical. This is the way I look at the Twelve Step groups for sex addicts. These people, though they may believe differently theologically, can save your life. They can help keep you from acting out which could kill you or end your marriage or destroy your family altogether. This addiction could kill you without support. Support groups are the life jackets.

If you have tried and tried again and failed, the life jackets could be the missing piece in your recovery to get and maintain sobriety. The people in this group can help you as you go through your steps and get rid of your guilt and shame and move forward to a life of whole living.

Seeing the Problem as a Triune Issue

As we discussed earlier in the book, sex addiction is a triune issue. It may have biological, psychological, and spiritual factors. If you are a Christian, (you have accepted Christ as your Lord and Savior) and have been genuine in that commitment, and it has evidenced itself in your life through prayer, Bible reading, and church attendance, and you find yourself still struggling with sex addiction, you probably, like myself, have lived in a world of confusion and self-loathing wondering if God could ever love you or use you at all.

This reminds me of a story when I first came to the Lord. I went to a nondenominational church and talked with a singles pastor. I told him I was struggling with masturbation. It was one of the most difficult times that I asked for help. This pastor told me to "just stop doing it!" That wasn't a solution for me. I spent four more years in my addiction because of the inadequacy of that conversation. I was reading more of the Bible than most people as I was in Bible school at the time. I would fast and pray for days and yet this addiction still had a grip in my life.

For me, part of my addiction was biological, which I didn't know at that point. The other part of my addiction was psychological. I wasn't aware that sex abuse and the abandonment of my father and mother had caused so much pain that I needed the medicine of sex addiction to aid my daily existence. If the possibility of this addiction can be a combination of biological, psychological and spiritual factors, it is a real possibility that you are going to need more than one solution.

Those who just want to use their Christianity to mask this addiction find themselves again and again falling flat on their faces, not being accountable and healed. Just talking to Jesus about the behavior and being forgiven for the behavior (I John 1:9) alone is ineffective. I have experienced the failure of that. I have been forgiven over and over again. The issue is that I was not healed. James 5:16 states that if we confess our faults one to another, we may be healed. "We may be healed" is very important. I needed healing from sexual addiction, not just forgiveness. The support groups can offer this to us. They can help us be accountable to someone, be honest about our thought life and behavior, and get healed. As we walk in that light and accountability, we can have healing from sex addiction.   It is a process, not an instantaneous moment though many of us have begged for that.

Spiritual language and principles need to be integrated into our recovery such as the basic principles of confession, honesty, open-mindedness and willingness in a community of people who want to do the same. The support group offers that safety for recovering sex addicts. After you have walked a year or so of sobriety and you feel that you want to start a support group in your church, that would be wonderful. I would encourage you to attend support groups first, however, before you intend to lead anyone into recovery.

Being Restored to God, Yourself and Others

As sex addicts, many have felt confused about their walk with God and their worthiness to be used by Him. They may feel that they are undeserving of His love because they fail, and when they fail, it seems they fail miserably. It is one thing to speed or lie, it is another to go into sexual behavior, especially when it involves others. It is confusing, overwhelming, and you can feel abandoned by yourself and God. God hasn't abandoned us. In recovery, we can have the kind of relationship that we have always wanted, and that is the relationship of a clean conscience. Paul talks a lot about the clear conscience in the New Testament. The way to have a clear conscience is through being honest, open, and confessing where we are with an accountable person or group, and usually that will be a support group of recovering sex addicts. Your wife at this point is definitely NOT who you need to be accountable to. You need a man if you are a man and a woman if you are a woman to be accountable to. The steps, especially Step Four through Step

Nine, are cleansers of the conscience and you can receive a lot of healing in completing the principles of these steps within your life.

Being restored to God will allow you to feel His presence with an integrity that you have never known before, because of the core belief, "If you really knew me, you wouldn't love me." This belief doesn't just apply to other people. Often times the sex addict applies it to God as well. Although He does know and love us, we are not able to feel that love at times because of where we are in our sexual addiction.

Being restored to yourself is part of having a clear conscience and knowing that today and maybe many days you have not done anything inappropriate or sinful sexually. It is a real reaccepting of yourself because for many sex addicts, they have abandoned themselves to their addiction. This is not the way it should be, but in our addiction, our life has become unmanageable. As we listen to others and ourselves in the recovering community, we can find a place where we can begin to put back the pieces, believe that we can accept ourselves the way we are, and that we are sex addicts and recovering. We can accept that we can do these principles and the work involved in it, and we can receive the healing God has intended for us. We can be restored and follow the second commandment of loving our neighbors as ourselves. If we loved people in our addiction, the way we loved ourselves, very few people would be in our lives.

Others

Being restored to others is a process of attending Twelve Step support groups, being accountable, honest, open-minded, and learning. In integrating these principles, you begin to have less shame, feel more lovable, and feel that you can walk into a group and be accepted and loved. You won't feel that if you get too close to people, they will find out you have a secret closet. When the closet has been opened and exposed, it will not have the same pain and power it did in the past. Being restored to others and developing close relationships is part of the process. The recovering community is where we can learn about intimacy, honesty and integrity in relationships. Those themes we have not been able to learn as deeply as we could because of our addiction. The recovering community can be a great instrument in being restored to God, ourselves and others.

People as a Part of the Process

In my experience, I have found that God uses people. In the New Testament, since the resurrection of Christ, an interesting thing has transpired. He personally did not heal anyone after His Resurrection. Instead the power of healing was transferred to the body of Christ. In the book of Acts, God used the apostles to heal those who were crippled, lame or had evil spirits. He used the body of Christ to heal one another, and it is in the body of Christ that we are going to find healing. There are many Christians in Twelve-Step Groups because we are convicted of our behavior. Others know that their behavior is inappropriate and will eventually seek help or eventually get exposed and then get help.

People in recovery know this addiction. They have fallen many times. They have danced with the same addiction that you have. They have done war and lost. But they have also won. They have called one another and encouraged each other. These are the people we need to be around. God uses people as a part of the healing process. In any area I was growing, God used people who had something that I needed so that I could learn. Many who have the information you need are in recovery groups because, with few exceptions, the church does not have the information to offer what recovering groups do at this time. I am hoping that this book is an instrument for change in that direction, and my prayer is that the church will open its doors to recovering sex addicts. If the church would do so, not only could it heal its own, but also it could begin to heal the community that is so affected. This would be no less than a revival.

Humility

As Christians, we talk a lot about humility, and yet know little about it. Like every other human being, I don't like the characteristics of humility. It is often painful. I have learned that basically there are two paths to humility. The first path is clear. We can humble ourselves.

Humbling ourselves in sexual addiction recovery can mean reading, praying, calling people, going to meetings, and praying again. Completing the exercises in this book, Integrating the principles and humbling ourselves will begin the healing process. Humbling ourselves in the sex addiction process may be going to a meeting where we may not believe 100 percent of another person's theology and yet listening to them. It may be listening to someone who has more sobriety than you and yet is younger than you. It can take on many facets as you recover from sexual addiction. I would have never dreamed that twenty-one years ago when God started speaking to me about sexual addiction (before books or support groups were available), that He would give me the basics. I did them. I had to humble myself, which was a very painful experience. I had to tell a pastor and a roommate about my sexual addiction, which was humbling. I didn't know that years later God would open doors internationally and I would share that testimony of personal recovery as to what works. I encourage you to humble yourself. It is the least painful way to humility.

The second road to humility is what I call humiliation. It is in this process that God will allow these principles to be exposed. This is when the sex addict gets caught with pornography by this spouse, or is accused of sexual misconduct at work, or caught in an extramarital affair. He gets exposed. We have seen this happen on a local level, and nationally. The humiliation wasn't for anything but for God to move the addict into recovery. If the person who is humiliated in this manner will move into recovery, God can begin to restore and replace what they need. Humiliation is much more painful and devastating and can take much longer to get over than simply humbling ourselves.

Humility is a key element to recovery. You cannot remain proud and succeed in going to groups and talking about your thought life. Humbling ourselves is much better than humiliation because once the humiliation experience has taken affect, the pain can be overwhelming. God is not concerned about whether we humble ourselves or get humiliated, as much as He is the result: that we are humble and learn how to recover. Either one is compassionate. It is compassion toward us if we humble ourselves and do what we need to do to recover, so that we can heal. And it is also compassionate of God to allow us to be exposed and heal. To keep someone in their addiction for years is the cruelest thing to let happen. So God, in His mercy, will humiliate us so that we can get to the bottom quicker and to recovery as soon as possible.

Outcome Is Worth the Input

Recovery is a front loaded investment. It is where we are going to have to do the maximum to get recovery. If you, as a Christian, can go to the Twelve Step group meetings, listen and learn, grow, get accountable, stay open-minded, honest, and gain sobriety, it is worth being restored to a clear conscience. Many have inherited much of what we are dealing with. I know that my father was at least an alcoholic and a sex addict. I inherited those things, but have been given a great opportunity to get healed. My prayer is that my children will not have this inheritance in their lives. The outcome of going to groups, doing the steps and getting into therapy is a testimony that many people need. There are a lot of people out there who don't know how to get healed from sexual addiction. If you get the input in, you will find a ministry and the joy that is definitely worth the journey. I experience so much joy seeing the changes in many people's lives because of the input God put in so that He can get the outcome He wants also. He wants it for you too. I hope that looking at the Twelve Step support groups differently can get you past any spiritual pettiness, so that you don't miss the blessing for yourself, your marriage, your entire family and your children's children.

If you feel that you need a Christian support group, you can start a Freedom Group in your church. Below is information on these groups and how to start one. Freedom groups were started by Heart to Heart Counseling Centers. Call our counseling center as you start them in your churches so that we can inform others that they are available in your area.

What are Freedom Groups?

Freedom Groups are Christ-based support groups for people wanting freedom from being sexually driven.

How do they work?

One man impressed by the Holy Spirit who wants to assist in helping others get freedom from being sexually driven asks his pastor to sponsor this ministry. This pointman will be the contact person for the church. The church will refer people who feel sexually driven to the pointman. This pointman will meet with those desiring help and will cover the Freedom Principles and Freedom Covenant (see next page) with them. Once the person agrees to the Freedom Principles and Freedom Covenant, they are given the group location and time.

Freedom Group Roles

1. The pointman serves as contact person for anyone to be brought into the group. This is to protect the group from someone just dropping in on the group. The point man can serve for an indefinite amount of time but should be reconsidered after one year of service.

2. The chairperson of the meeting is responsible to start the meeting by asking the pointman if any new people need to make a Freedom Covenant. If there are no new Freedom Covenants to be addressed, the chairperson starts the introductions (see Freedom Meetings) and chooses the topic for the group discussion. The chairperson serves the group for a maximum of 8 weeks. At that time someone else volunteers to chair the meeting.

Freedom Principles: First 100 Days of Recovery

1. Pray: Pray in the morning asking God to keep you free today.
2. Read: Read the Bible and read freedom-related material.
3. Call: Call someone in your group and check in with that person at the beginning of each day.
4. Meetings: Attend every meeting possible.
5. Pray: Pray in the evening thanking God for keeping you free today.

One-Year Freedom Covenant

1. The members of the Freedom Group covenant to total confidentiality of all group members and discussions held during group meetings.
2. Members covenant to attend the Freedom Group for one year and to work through the Freedom Materials and report progress to the group.
3. Members covenant to keep the Freedom Principles for the first 100 days of their journey toward freedom.

Freedom Meetings

1. Any new members are introduced by the pointman and are asked to verbalize the Freedom Covenant to the group in the first person. (Example: I covenant to...)
2. Introductions: Beginning with the chairperson of the meeting, introductions are done as follows: The chairperson introduces himself, shares his feelings, shares his boundaries and length of time free from those behaviors. (Example: "My name is John. I feel frustrated and alone. My boundaries to stay free are no pornography, bookstores, and no sex outside of marriage. I worked on Exercises #5-#7 in my 101 Freedom Exercises workbook and made four pages of progress on my Steps to Freedom workbook since our last meeting. I have been free for 3 weeks.")
3. The chairperson chooses a topic related to staying free from being sexually driven that the group discusses.   Each   member can share without feedback from the group, unless feedback is specifically asked for by the sharing member.

4. Honest Time: Group members pair off into 2-3 members and discuss thoughts, behaviors, struggles, and successes since the last meeting (James 5:16).
5. Closing Prayer: Group members get back together and repeat the Lord's Prayer together.

Freedom Group Materials

1. The Final Freedom: Pioneering Sex Addiction Recovery - This title comes in a 5 CD series or book. In addition to informing sex addicts and their partners about sex addiction, it gives hope for recovery.

2. 101 Practical Exercises: A Guide To Sex Addiction Recovery - This workbook contains 101 proven techniques that Dr. Weiss has used to successfully help thousands obtain and maintain their sexual addiction recovery. This is a great follow-up tool to The Final Freedom.

3. Steps To Freedom: A Christian 12-Step Guide For Sexual Addiction - This is a thorough interaction with the Twelve-Steps of recovery. This workbook was designed to be used in a group setting but can be used individually also.

These materials and others can be ordered from Heart to Heart Counseling Center by the options listed in the Resource Section in Appendix D. Groups ordering ten or more of one item can call for a group discount.

Freedom Group Topics for Discussion

Triggers	Honesty	Fear
Hope	Bottom Lines	Relapse
Control	H.A.L.T.	Steps 1-12
Boundaries	Prayer	Maximized Thinking
Recovery Rituals	Feelings	Anger
Dangerous Dabbling	Fun	Father Issues
Sexual Abuse	Objectifying	Grooming Victims

Accountability	Discipline	Acts of Love
My Calling	My Future	Daily Struggles
Dangerous Places	What Works	Dating My Wife
Control	Male Friends	Humility
Turning It Over	God's Grace	One Day at a Time
My Daily God Time	Discipline	My Worst Moment
The Gift of Recovery	Intimacy	Breaking the Curse for My Children
What God is Doing	Exercise	Addictions in My Family

...And any other topic the chairperson feels is appropriate. Remember, don't be graphic, be honest!

APPENDIX

FEELINGS LIST

1. I feel (put word here) when (put a present situation when you feel this).
2. I first remember feeling (put the same feeling word here) when (explain earliest occurrence of this feeling).

Rules For Couples: 1- No examples about each other or the relationship. 2-Eye contact. 3-No feedback

Abandoned	Aware	Close	Deprived	Feisty
Abused	Awestruck	Cold	Deserted	Ferocious
Aching	Badgered	Comfortable	Desirable	Foolish
Accepted	Baited	Comforted	Desired	Forced
Accused	Bashful	Competent	Despair	Forceful
Accepting	Battered	Competitive	Despondent	Forgiven
Admired	Beaten	Complacent	Destroyed	Forgotten
Adored	Beautiful	Complete	Different	Free
Adventurous	Belligerent	Confident	Dirty	Friendly
Affectionate	Belittled	Confused	Disenchanted	Frightened
Agony	Bereaved	Considerate	Disgusted	Frustrated
Alienated	Betrayed	Consumed	Disinterested	Full
Aloof	Bewildered	Content	Dispirited	Funny
Aggravated	Blamed	Cool	Distressed	Furious
Agreeable	Blaming	Courageous	Distrustful	Gay
Aggressive	Bonded	Courteous	Distrusted	Generous
Alive	Bored	Coy	Disturbed	Grouchy
Alone	Bothered	Crabby	Dominated	Grumpy
Alluring	Brave	Cranky	Domineering	Hard
Amazed	Breathless	Crazy	Doomed	Harried
Amused	Bristling	Creative	Doubtful	Hassled
Angry	Broken-up	Critical	Dreadful	Healthy
Anguished	Bruised	Criticized	Eager	Helpful
Annoyed	Bubbly	Cross	Ecstatic	Helpless
Anxious	Burdened	Crushed	Edgy	Hesitant
Apart	Burned	Cuddly	Edified	High
Apathetic	Callous	Curious	Elated	Hollow
Apologetic	Calm	Cut	Embarrassed	Honest
Appreciated	Capable	Damned	Empowered	Hopeful
Appreciative	Captivated	Dangerous	Empty	Hopeless
Apprehensive	Carefree	Daring	Enraged	Horrified
Appropriate	Careful	Dead	Enraptured	Hostile
Approved	Careless	Deceived	Enthusiastic	Humiliated
Argumentative	Caring	Deceptive	Enticed	Hurried
Aroused	Cautious	Defensive	Esteemed	Hurt
Astonished	Certain	Delicate	Exasperated	Hyper
Assertive	Chased	Delighted	Excited	Ignorant
Attached	Cheated	Demeaned	Exhilarated	Joyous
Attacked	Cheerful	Demoralized	Exposed	Lively
Attentive	Childlike	Dependent	Fake	Lonely
Attractive	Choked Up	Depressed	Fascinated	Loose

Lost	Pulled apart	Sexy	Tight	Whole
Loving	Put down	Shattered	Timid	Wicked
Low	Puzzled	Shocked	Tired	Wild
Lucky	Quarrelsome	Shot down	Tolerant	Willing
Lustful	Queer	Shy	Tormented	Wiped out
Mad	Quiet	Sickened	Torn	Wishful
Maudlin	Raped	Silly	Tortured	Withdrawn
Malicious	Ravished	Sincere	Touched	Wonderful
Mean	Ravishing	Sinking	Trapped	Worried
Miserable	Real	Smart	Tremendous	Worthy
Misundertstood	Refreshed	Smothered	Tricked	
Moody	Regretful	Smug	Trusted	
Morose	Rejected	Sneaky	Trustful	
Mournful	Rejuvenated	Snowed	Trusting	
Mystified	Rejecting	Soft	Ugly	
Nasty	Relaxed	Solid	Unacceptable	
Nervous	Relieved	Solitary	Unapproachable	
Nice	Remarkable	Sorry	Unaware	
Numb	Remembered	Spacey	Uncertain	
Nurtured	Removed	Special	Uncomfortable	
Nuts	Repulsed	Spiteful	Under control	
Obsessed	Repulsive	Spontaneous	Understanding	
Offended	Resentful	Squelched	Understood	
Open	Resistant	Starved	Undesirable	
Ornery	Responsible	Stiff	Unfriendly	
Out of control	Responsive	Stimulated	Ungrateful	
Overcome	Repressed	Stifled	Unified	
Overjoyed	Respected	Strangled	Unhappy	
Overpowered	Restless	Strong	Unimpressed	
Overwhelmed	Revolved	Stubborn	Unsafe	
Pampered	Riled	Stuck	Unstable	
Panicked	Rotten	Stunned	Upset	
Paralyzed	Ruined	Stupid	Uptight	
Paranoid	Sad	Subdued	Used	
Patient	Safe	Submissive	Useful	
Peaceful	Satiated	Successful	Useless	
Pensive	Satisfied	Suffocated	Unworthy	
Perceptive	Scared	Sure	Validated	
Perturbed	Scolded	Sweet	Valuable	
Phony	Scorned	Sympathy	Valued	
Pleasant	Scrutinized	Tainted	Victorious	
Pleased	Secure	Tearful	Violated	
Positive	Seduced	Tender	Violent	
Powerless	Seductive	Tense	Voluptuous	
Present	Self-centered	Terrific	Vulnerable	
Precious	Self-conscious	Terrified	Warm	
Pressured	Selfish	Thrilled	Wary	
Pretty	Separated	Ticked	Weak	
Proud	Sensuous	Tickled	Whipped	

Guideline #1:
No Examples
About Each Other

Guideline #2:
Maintain Eye
Contact

Guideline #3:
No Feedback

The Twelve-Steps of Alcoholics Anonymous
Adapted for Sexual Addicts

1. We admitted we were powerless over our spouse's intimacy anorexia and that our lives had become unmanageable.

2. Came to believe that a Power greater than ourselves could restore us to sanity.

3. Made a decision to turn our will and our lives over to the care of God as we understood Him.

4. Made a searching and fearless moral inventory of ourselves.

5. Admitted to God, to ourselves, and to another human being the exact nature of our wrongs.

6. Were entirely ready to have God remove all these defects of character.

7. Humbly asked God to remove our shortcomings.

8. Made a list of all people we had harmed, and became willing to make amends to them all.

9. Made direct amends to such people wherever possible, except when to do so would injure them or others.

10. Continued to take personal inventory, and when we were wrong, promptly admitted it.

11. Sought through prayer and meditation to improve our conscious contact with God as we understood Him, praying only for knowledge of His will for us and the power to carry that out.

12. Having had a spiritual awakening as the result of these steps, we tried to carry this message to others and to practice these principles in all our day to day living.

MEN'S RECOVERY

This book gives more current information than many professional counselors have today on sexual addiction. $22.95

This workbook will outline the best techniques to help obtain freedom from sexual addiction. $39.95

This step book is specifically written for the person desiring recovery from sexual addiction. $14.95

Offers practical tools for hearing her pain, navigating her grief and losses, discovering her expectations of you and the boundaries she may need to heal. $69.95

This CD will give you more information than most therapists have on sexual addiction. You will be able to finally know how you became a sexual addict and identify why you might still be relapsing. $29.95

Once you know the type of sex addict you are, Dr. Doug outlines the same treatment plan you would receive in an individual session. $29.95

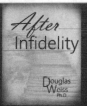  

Helps identify key points about the whys of infidelity, the types of cheaters, and how to start walking toward a healthy marriage. $49.95

This amazing DVD has 8 addicts telling their stories through directed questions. These individuals address key issues along with their journey through recovery. $19.95

Making Amends was created for men who are working through their sexual addiction recovery and have reached Step 9 where they make amends to their wife. $19.95

www.drdougweiss.com 719.278.3708

INTIMACY ANOREXIA

This hidden addiction is destroying so many marriages today. In your hands is the first antidote for a person or spouse with anorexia to turn the pages on this addiction process. $22.95

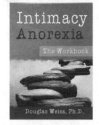

This is like therapy in a box. Inside is 100 exercises that have already been proven helpful in treating intimacy anorexia. $39.95

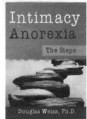

This is the only twelve step workbook just for intimacy anorexia. Each step gives you progress in your healing from intimacy anorexia. $14.95

This book will not only unlock the understanding of intimacy anorexia but you will also hear experiences of spouses who have found themselves married and alone. $14.95

This is the first workbook to offer practical suggestions and techniques to better navigate through recovery from your spouse's Intimacy Anorexia. $39.95

These Steps can further your healing and recovery from your spouse's Intimacy Anorexia. $14.95

This DVD will give you the characteristics, causes and strategies of intimacy anorexia. This DVD also provides solutions for the intimacy anorexic to start their road to recovery. $69.95

This DVD is for the spouse of an intimacy/sexual anorexic. Dr. Weiss will help you to start a journey of recovery from living with a spouse with intimacy anorexia. $49.95

www.drdougweiss.com 719.278.3708

WOMEN'S RECOVERY

This book offers the readers hope, along with a plan for recovery. Any woman who is a partner of a sex addict will find this book a necessity for her journey toward healing. $14.95

This is like therapy in a box for women who want to walk through the residual effects of being in a relationship with a sex addict. $39.95

This is an interactive workbook that allows the partners of sex addicts to gain insight and strength through working the Twelve Steps. $14.95

This DVD set is for any woman who is currently or was in a relationship with a sexual addict. If anger is still an issue, this material can help with her healing. $29.95

In this DVD set Dr. Weiss will expose the viewer to specific reasons as to why men lie and helpful strategies to end the lying. $44.95

In 90-minutes, this DVD answers the ten most frequently asked questions for partners of sex addicts. $69.95

This amazing DVD has 8 partners of sex addicts telling their stories through directed questions. A must DVD for every spouse of a sex addict. $19.95

This 2 hour DVD set was produced for divorced women who desire to date again. $29.95

This set deals with partner issues of an addict. This is a religious focus and gives biblical answers to boundaries, tough love and how to love an addict effectively the way God does. $38.00

OTHER RESOURCES

"Born for War" teaches practical tools to defeat these sexual landmines and offers scriptural truths that empower young men to desire successfulness in the war thrust upon them. $29.95

This 2 hour DVD helps single women ages 15-30, to successfully navigate through the season of dating. $29.95

This 2 Disc DVD Series is definitely nothing you have heard before. Dr. Weiss charts new territory as to the why for sexual purity. $29.95

A gift for your daugher as she enters college. Letters to my Daughter includes my daily letters to my daughter during her first year of college. $14.95

Erin discovers she comes from a long line of dragons, dragons who have effectively maintained Earth's balance since the planet's beginning. Will she accept her fate and responsibility? $14.95

This DVD contains a straight-forward sex talk for Christian men, shattering common myths about male sexuality and male sexual addiction. $29.95

This DVD is essential in undertaking the role of spiritual and practical intersession for individuals, churches, cities or nation. $19.95

This book is the most current book in the field of sex addiction for women and is packed with new statistics to further our understanding of female sexual addiction. $14.95

This is the most solution-oriented and practical workbook for female sexual addiction to date. $39.95

www . d r d o u g w e i s s . c o m   7 1 9 . 2 7 8 . 3 7 0 8

COUNSELING

"Without the intensive, my marriage would have ended and I would not have known why. Now I am happier than ever and my marriage is bonded permanently."

Counseling Sessions

Couples are helped through critical phases of disclosure moving into the process of recovery, and rebuilding trust in relationships. We have helped many couples rebuild their relationship and grasp and implement the necessary skills for an intimate relationship.

Individual counseling offers a personal treatment plan for successful healing in your life. In just one session a counselor can help you understand how you became stuck and how to move toward freedom.

Partners of sex addicts need an advocate. Feelings of fear, hurt, anger, betrayal, and grief require a compassionate, effective response. We provide that expert guidance and direction. We have helped many partners heal through sessions that get them answers to their many questions including: "How can I trust him again?"

A counseling session today can begin your personal journey toward healing.

3 and 5 Day Intensives

in Colorado Springs, Colorado
are available for the following issues:

- Sexual Addiction Couple or Individual
- Marriage Intensives
- Partners of Sexual Addicts
- Intimacy Anorexia
- Victims of Sexual Abuse
- Adult Children of Sex Addicts
- Teenage Children of Sex Addicts
- Teen Intensive

Attendees of Intensives will receive:

- Personal attention from counselors who specialize in your area of need
- An understanding of how the addiction /anorexia and its consequences came into being
- Three appointments daily
- Daily assignments to increase the productiveness of these daily sessions
- Individuals get effective counseling to recover from the effects of sexual addiction, abuse and anorexia
- Addiction, abuse, anorexia issues are thoroughly addressed for couples and individuals. This includes the effects on the partner or family members of the addict, and how to rebuild intimacy toward a stronger relationship.